SO-BOB-809

Dreaming *of* Columbus

New York City History and Culture
Jay Kaplan, *Series Editor*

Dreaming *of* Columbus

A BOYHOOD IN THE BRONX

Michael Pearson

SYRACUSE UNIVERSITY PRESS

Copyright © 1999 by Syracuse University Press

Syracuse, New York 13244-5160

All Rights Reserved

First Edition 1999

99   00   01   02   03   04   6   5   4   3   2   1

Some of the names in this book have been changed to protect individual privacy. Otherwise, the author kept to the facts as accurately as research and memory allow.

The paper used in this publication meets the minimum requirements of American National Standard for Information Sciences—Permanence of Paper for Printed Library Materials, ANSI Z39.48-1984. ∞™

Library of Congress Cataloging-in-Publication Data

Pearson, Michael, 1949–

> Dreaming of Columbus : a boyhood in the Bronx / Michael Pearson.—
> 1st ed.
>
>> p.   cm.—(New York City history and culture)
>
> ISBN 0-8156-0561-7 (cloth : alk. paper)
>
>> 1. Pearson, Michael, 1949–   —Childhood and youth.   2. Bronx (New
> York, N.Y.)—Biography.   3. New York (N.Y.)—Biography.   4. Irish
> Americans—New York (State)—New York—Social life and customs.
> 5. Irish Americans—New York (State)—New York—Biography.
> I. Title   II. Series : New York City (Syracuse, N.Y.)
> F128.68.B8P33   1999
> 974.7'275043'092—dc21
> [B]   98-38554

Manufactured in the United States of America

· ·

Dreaming of Columbus is a work of nonfiction, a blend of memoir and reportage. It is the story of a place, the Bronx; a time, principally the 1960s; and a culture, mainly Irish Catholic. In part, it is also a description of the Bronx today, an attempt to discover how the past might lead to the present, our dreams creating our memories, and how what we seek might find us, allowing our memories to re-create our dreams.

This book is dedicated to Dorothy, Marion, Virginia, and always Jo-Ellen, for even though this is a tale of a boyhood, these women deeply affected the story and make the Bronx—however dingy, gray, smog covered—seem radiant and alive to me even today.

Michael Pearson is the director of creative writing at Old Dominion University and the author of three other books. *Imagined Places: Journeys into Literary America* was listed by the *New York Times Book Review* as a Notable Book of 1992. His other books are *John McPhee,* a biographical-critical study, and *A Place That's Known,* a collection of essays.

So you dream of Columbus
Every time that the panic starts
You dream of Columbus
With your maps and your beautiful charts
You dream of Columbus
With an ache in your traveling heart.

—NOEL BRAZIL, "Columbus"
(as sung by Mary Black)

Contents

···

PART ONE

Rest *in* Peace

*Rip's story was soon told, for the whole twenty years
had been to him but as one night.*

—Washington Irving,
"Rip Van Winkle"

*I could be Rip Van Winkle. Only I thought that the
Rip Van Winkle story was all wrong. You went to
sleep for a long time and when you woke up nothing
whatsoever had changed. No matter how long you
slept, it was the same.*

—Robert Penn Warren,
All the King's Men

A Bronx Legend —
How Rip Got His Name

The shapes of things changed in the summertime.
The smoke from the hat factory next door became fat
and slow, oozing like a chorus of fat ladies in pink,
blue, yellow, purple dresses.

—Kate Simon, *Bronx Primitive*

In the summertime the Bronx was filled with dreams. The days
flowed indiscernibly, a sluggish stream, one day moving unnoticed
into the next, all part of the long, lazy drift of time. The apartment
buildings, rectangles of frozen brick in the winter, seemed to thaw
and then sway in the shimmering summer heat. Faces softened,
people slowed their gaits, and children sat in slivers of shade on the
stoops, imagining their golden futures. Even the sweat-soaked
adults who plodded back across the Grand Concourse in the early
evening after exiting the trains had a look of dreamy contemplation.
Everyone appeared to be thinking of another place, another time.

We were fourteen years old and uncertain what our dreams
should be, what dreams were any longer possible, but we roamed
in packs like wild-eyed wolves, at turns loping and lethargic, need-
ing each other's company, but never sure why.

It was a June day in 1964, seven months after the murder of John F. Kennedy, and the sun burned down on the Bronx. The air turned thick and sullen, workers slumped resignedly in their subway seats, and playgrounds looked bleached and useless. The atmosphere was so heavy that it seemed opaque and the future impossibly distant.

On that day, Thomas Slater lost his name and found a new one.

Slater hung out with a crowd from Bainbridge Avenue, a group of boys that gathered along the metal fence railing that stretched the length of Mosholu Parkway. They perched there like birds on a wire, staring at the stone wall of P.S. 8 and at the empty playground beyond it, sighing and hoping for some threat or seduction. On that day, there seemed little chance of either.

Elbows resting on knees, chins cupped in their palms, the five boys sat, waiting. In a way they looked as if they were half formed, pieces to be fitted together. Vinnie they called "Pork": he was short and fat, but the nickname may have had more to do with the bristly hairs covering his body, jutting out like quills even in the moist air, than with his slovenly eating habits. Nevertheless, as he sat there, the sun glinted off shiny streams of mustard and chocolate ice cream that veined his shirt. Fitz, who was a head taller than Pork, sat next to him, one hand feeling his tensed tricep, the other fondly massaging his crotch. Johnny was called "Fleas," but no one had even a remote idea why. He was all angles and smirks, proud of the fact that he had never been caught saying a serious word since he was in the fifth grade. Al was small and blond, a year younger than the rest and a few years wiser, with the face of an altar boy. Tommy Slater sat slumped next to him, and of all the boys he appeared the most unfinished. His limbs were as thin as pipe stems. His reddish-brown hair had the texture of a Brillo pad and the shape of a dented hubcap. His green eyes popped out just enough to give him a slight but permanently dazed expression, and his freckled mouth twisted ironically, a combination that made people see him as arrogant and simple-minded at the same time.

No one was sure exactly what to make of him. He was odd, but his oddities were not easily defined. Therefore, he remained un-named, except for the ordinary "Tom" given to him by his parents. But these ordinary names meant little to most of us who had spent eight years at St. Philip Neri Elementary School together. Names like Natty Bumppo or Bruce Wayne held little value, but Hawkeye or Batman were laced with meaning. Names were earned, but for us they were rarely badges of honor. So, along with the generic as-sociations—greaseball, potato eater, yiddle—were the personal namings: Frankie Bartoletti was Bart the Fart, Johnny DeCaprio was Johnny Mizer, and Steve Tarnok was Levite. We knew a little about basic human instincts, a lot about bodily functions, and we had even learned something about the Old Testament in those years at St. Philip's. Those names and others were sometimes picked up for small misdeeds, for being in the wrong place at the wrong time, but most often they were earned, like a scarlet letter, for the unpardonable sin—failing to be inconspicuous. Our Bronx was the Catholic Bronx, our apartments looked alike, our prayers went up in the same Latin bursts to God; we were taught silence and obedience, to learn by rote, to stand quietly in line, to be part of the flock.

Despite his alien hairdo and bemused look, Thomas Slater was inconspicuous, as indistinguishable as one sheep from another. In his eight years at St. Philip's, he was always known as Tommy, or he was barely recognized at all. In the eighth-grade class there were fifty-four boys, seated not according to height or alphabetical order, but according to academic ability. This left Slater in the last row, along the edge of the room, by the jalousie windows, gazing out at the buses and cars on the boulevard. His daydreams took him any-where but into math and history, and he was rarely snapped out of his slack-jawed ruminations because Brother Bruce and Brother Placid had more interesting cases to hold their attention.

Behind Slater sat three or four boys who seemed to defy all but the most inventive definitions of obtuseness. Even Brother Boniface, who always seemed ready to believe in all forms of depravity and stupidity, was at times pleasantly surprised by the amorphous dullness he discovered in Jimmy Keane and John Knecht, who competed for the last seat in the last row. These two young men were capable of forgetting how to spell *cat*, would not always associate Christmas Day and December 25, and might not be able to say who was buried in Grant's Tomb. Deep down, Brother Boniface loved them for the opportunities for sarcasm they provided. For him, they were a source of unending sadistic joy. Most of us appreciated Keane and Knecht, too, but for different reasons. We saw them as some sort of pod people: they inhabited our world without ever seeming to take the same desperate interest in it that we did. And, more important to us, they took most of the attention that we didn't want. We had learned our religious lessons well—they were our smiling martyrs.

Tommy Slater was not that dull and probably not that good-natured, either. Compared with Jimmy Keane he seemed to be a thinker as profound as Søren Kierkegaard. Compared with John Knecht, who smoked two packs of Chesterfields a day, drank a few beers on the weekends, had been left back three times, and appeared withered before the bloom of the confirmation slap was off his cheek in the fourth grade, Slater was nearly handsome. He was not an athlete, but he didn't compound that error by being studious as well. For all practical purposes he was unnoticed. He didn't exist. He slipped from one grade to another without anyone's paying much attention, always near the top of the last row, anonymous, a boy with no future but with no past either.

On that June day Tommy sat on the metal fence along Mosholu Parkway, eyes narrowed in the sunlight, and no one was more surprised than he, it seemed, when he broke the silence.

"Shit, this is boring," he said, nearly falling off the railing as if the words tripped a delicate balance.

No one appeared to hear him. Nobody turned a head in his direction.

"Let's go to the RKO Fordham," Fleas suggested. "I hear they got *Topkapi* playing there. It's advertised on all the buses."

"What the hell's *Topkapi?*" Pork asked. "*My Fair Lady*'s playing at the Loew's Paradise. . . ." Before the words had even fully formed as sound, Pork realized he had made a mistake, said something foolish, made himself conspicuous. But it was too late. Fitz started the onslaught:

"*My Fair Lady*, eh, Pork? I bet you'd *love* to see that. Anything to do with fairies, huh?"

For the next few minutes Pork's masculinity was loudly called into question. But much of the conversation was a ritual, a sort of irreligious litany, a familiar chant and response that went this way:

"Suck on it."

"Whip it out."

"You wish I would."

"You couldn't find it."

"You're such a faggot."

"You wish I was."

"I know."

"You blow."

"You wish I did."

"You wish you could."

"You couldn't even find it."

"Your mother found it."

Usually when someone's mother was invoked, it signaled the end of the conversation. It meant the boys were running out of ideas. The ultimate disgrace was not stupidity, lack of coordination, or even effeminacy, but rather any question of a mother's virtue. The word *mother* foreshadowed the end of the discussion, but before a shoving match or the metallic challenge of zipper opening, the boys' attention turned to a Volkswagen rattling up to the stop sign.

The driver turned toward them, a flash of long hair, yellow beard, unfocused eyes. His radio was just loud enough for Peter, Paul, and Mary's "Blowing in the Wind" to drift incongruously into the Angels' whining "My boyfriend's back and there's gonna be trouble," which came from an apartment across the street where two young girls were practicing the Watusi and the Frug. The boys watched the Volkswagen sputter off, but none of them seemed to take notice of the clashing sounds. It was the year of the Beatles, but it was also the year of the Four Seasons, Bobby Vinton, and the Singing Nun.

After another half hour discussing all the possibilities—swimming at Tibbets Brook Pool in Yonkers, playing knock hockey at the rec center, having an egg cream at Lou and Arty's Candy Store—four of them were still stuck on the fence. Al had gone home. It was Pork, with a photographic memory for every movie theater timetable, who brought up the idea of going to see a porno movie in Manhattan. They decided on the World Theater on Forty-ninth Street between Eighth and Ninth Avenues. Tommy was the first one to lift himself from the fence. He had been sitting there backside on the top railing, feet on the lower railing, and head bent so that his body resembled a question mark. He straightened up, stretched, and the other boys did the same. But before they could screw their courage to the act, they got one of the older boys in the neighborhood to buy a six-pack of beer. They each drank one and shared the last two as they walked along the Bedford Park Boulevard underpass, a gaping passage that led to the Independent Subway line. Under the bridge, the whoosh of cars turned loud and threatening, and the filth seemed dark and sad. Scrawled over the entrance to the subway was the word "Beware," and right next to it, "Kiss my ass." The boys bounced the empty cans off the last two Ss, drops of beer splashing against the wall, the cans rattling into the road.

The subway station was gray and empty. Every sound echoed through the silence. In a rush, without planning it, the four of them jumped the turnstiles, laughing, leaping down the steps to the subway platform, barely hearing the deep, featureless voice from the booth, "Hey, you damned kids, get back here." The D train was screeching into the station, and they jumped on, pushing their way through to the first car.

Soon the gentle rocking of the subway car lulled them into a stillness. Their laughter became smiles, and their smiles turned to dull stares as they gazed out the front glass near the engineer's booth. The train careened through the tunnels, incandescent lights and flashing red and green signals occasionally piercing the darkness, in a frightening flash making it clear how close the walls were to the hurtling cars. It was a flickering psychedelic ride, darkness washing over them and the rhythmic clicks of the wheels spinning them backwards, it seemed, away from the world, the light, the present. By the time they reached Fiftieth Street and Sixth Avenue, they would have been content to keep riding the train indefinitely, remaining in a pleasant half-wakefulness. But one moved, then the next, and before they realized it, the sunlight struck them hard between the eyes. Each one raised his hand to ward off the blow.

Squint-eyed to the sun, they snaked their way through the lunch crowds near Rockefeller Plaza, past the skating rink, an iceless crater guarded by a golden Atlas, near Radio City Music Hall, where the dancers in old shorts and tattered T-shirts rehearsed for their evening performance, and across Broadway. On Eighth Avenue a gauntlet of prostitutes in tight red shorts and purple halters asked them with a genteel mockery if they would "like a date, honey." The boys smiled awkwardly, scared speechless by the used, skeletal faces in the stark daylight. They pushed on toward the side entrance to the movie theater as one of the prostitutes called to a young sailor across the street.

Fitz, who looked older than the rest, bought a ticket and headed for the side door after telling the usher that someone was getting sick in the bathroom. In an instant the other three were inside the unlit movie theater, invisible in the darkness. Only four or five seats were taken, but they sat in the next to last row, whispering, elbowing one another, their attention fixed on the movie in progress. They tried to appear nonchalant, making jokes and sarcastic remarks about the actors and actresses, but their hearts pounded, and their eyes were riveted to the screen, all dilating flesh.

The story concerned a group of women who had enslaved the men on their island, killing all but those who could perform with exceptional sexual dexterity. The plot was thin despite the allusion to mythology, but the action was thick and fast. Soon the boys' jokes stopped, and they lost track of one another in the dark heat of their own separate worlds. They also lost a hold on time amidst the moans and screams, and Fitz wasn't certain how long they had been there when he turned to his right and saw Tommy Slater slouched in his seat, his eyes apparently closed. Fitz nudged Pork and nodded to Fleas, who was just then emerging from his own smoky dreams. One of them reached over and waved a hand in front of Slater's face. Another snapped his fingers.

He was asleep. The boys couldn't quite believe their eyes: Slater had fallen asleep during a pornographic movie. If it could be explained by some spell or narcoleptic fit, they might have nudged him awake, but instead they slowly, quietly rose from their seats and made their way up the aisle, leaving him lying there like a kid who had dozed off at the end of geography class.

"Let's get out of here," one of them said, and before they could discuss it, they were running through the harsh daylight toward the train back to the Bronx. On the ride home they may have wondered what powerful drowsiness could have overcome him when all their senses were shot through with heat and blood, when the whole world seemed unendurably awake. They might have envied him the innocent dreams that could have accompanied such a sleep. When they returned to Bedford Park Station at 200th Street, they waited by the pizza place for a time, watching line after line of subway passengers pulse from the tunnel. As the sky turned from purple to black, they headed home, wondering, perhaps, if Slater would ever return to the Bronx.

He did, much later. Somehow he had lost one shoe, and from an apartment window one of the boys saw him as he limped along Bainbridge Avenue on a moonless night that seemed to cast shadows everywhere, changing the shapes of trees and buildings, changing even him.

By the next day he *was* someone else. He was no longer Tommy Slater, but Rip. No one was sure who coined the name, but it stuck so fast that in a few years many people who knew Rip had no idea what his legal name was. He had gone to sleep as Tommy Slater and awakened as Rip, a different person, from that moment conspicuous, the center of attention. He had been transformed by a few hours and would never be the same. Within a couple of years he was spending all of his nights at Darby O'Gill's Bar doing imitations of Mick Jagger or at a friend's house lounging lazily until the beer ran out. Then he would sit up, his skeletal frame rattling, and say, "Let's shoot out for some tastes."

It was as if he fell in love with being noticed. It was as if he fell in love with the sleep he had slipped into like a new country. He had brought back nothing but more dreams. Nevertheless, he had crossed some threshold, and the Bronx made us all think about moving on. All the roads seemed to lead away from what we knew, away from who we were. So, no matter how much we wanted to hold onto some fragment of our identity, we wanted even more to be transformed.

Of course, sometimes it's wise not to wish too much for certain things because occasionally we get what we want. Rip's smile began to tilt even more crazily, a postmodernist Cheshire grin. He got skinnier than his hero, Mick Jagger—even his lips seemed to swell. His hair bloomed wildly, mushrooming from his forehead like an atomic blast. Stories began to spring from him, flapping around him like paper butterflies in a cartoon. As the years went by, his friends went to college, but Rip became a legend. Despite the fact that he seemed to work off and on and date occasionally, he always had time to hang out with his friends, to drink a few beers, to drift along idly.

When he was twenty or so, he was arrested for pissing on the ground-level window of an elderly woman's apartment. She might have thought the water streaming against her kitchen window was an abrupt downpour, but Rip was also screaming out the lyrics to "Midnight Rambler" as he relieved himself. When the woman opened her blinds, she gasped at the jumble of images she saw—a wild man howling at the moon, a waterfall against her window, scuffed shoes, hairy appendages.

The cops arrived before he was fully zipped. When he was brought down to the station house, the desk sergeant told him, "You're being booked for Peeping Tommery." Rip smiled up at him sadly, held himself unsteadily against the desk, and said, "Thank you, sir. You're the first person who's called me Tom in years."

Shortly after that, rumor had it he came home one night and found a note stuck to the kitchen sink. His parents had moved to Florida. Supposedly, they forgot to leave him a forwarding address.

Perhaps he found them, though, because when I saw him again twenty years later, he was a sunbaked real estate salesman living in Florida, somewhere near St. Augustine. He mentioned the houses he owned, the deals he was making, the trips he took, but his clothes looked threadbare, his shoes worn thin, his eyes streaked with red. He reminded me of the Bronx, of those dream-laden summer days when we all gazed longingly into the distance. As he talked, one hand rested on his hip, the other pointed freely—one more imitation, it seemed to me, of Mick Jagger—and his eyelids looked heavy with an ambiguous memory, as if he had never fully awakened from some enigmatic sleep.

•••••

> The invisible hand of the Almighty Father surely
> guided me to this beautiful country, a land covered
> with virgin forest and unlimited opportunities. It is a
> veritable paradise and needs but the industrious
> hand of man to make it the finest and most beautiful
> region in the world.
>
> —Jonas Bronck, in a seventeenth-century
> letter to a friend in Europe

The Bronx is shaped like a fat man's heart, its forty-two square miles swelling into a bloated rectangle that leans toward City Island and the Long Island Sound in the east. The borough, which is roughly the same size as Paris, is known for its slums, its almost apocalyptic look of decay in places, but in its northwest corner in Riverdale there are landscaped suburbs and million-dollar estates. In one baronial mansion with a dining room sixty feet long and striking views of the steamboats coursing up and down the river in the shadow of the Palisades, Mark Twain, an unlikely resident of the Bronx, lived from 1901 to 1903. To the west, the Hudson River narrows from its wide swath near Haverstraw and Ossining and separates the Bronx from the cliffs of New Jersey. In the south, the Harlem River cuts it off from the island of Manhattan, from the thin slip of land most people think of when they say "New York City."

The Bronx is veined by roads, clogged with more than one million people, tens of thousands of apartment buildings, cars, buses, stores, but it is also a landscape of parks—the Bronx Zoo, the Botanical Gardens, Van Cortlandt, St. James—one hundred fifty of them, encompassing more than six thousand acres. Perhaps it is fitting that one quarter of all the land in the Bronx is park land, for at one time it was the frontier outside of the city of Manhattan. Then it became farm land. Wolves were thought to be one of the greatest threats in the area, and the Provincial Assembly offered thirty shillings for a grown wolf killed by a Christian, ten for one killed by an Indian. Wolf pits were once a common sight, as were deer, flocks of wild turkeys, and beaver dams. The Bronx was at one time a geography of heavy woodlands covering rolling hills and valleys, of streams and brooks rippling through fertile soil. Trees were cut by axe and adze, notched, made into trim log cabins by determined settlers. The Dutch built homes of stone, with ample kitchens and generous fireplaces. They walked across their muddy pastures, past cows and sheep, on their way to the Harlem River or the Sound to fish or into the cool, dark forest to hunt.

That world must seem unimaginable now, of course, to anyone standing near the boarded windows of storefronts or within sight of the rubble from a razed tenement in the once fashionable Highbridge section. Yet the Bronx is still the northernmost section of New York City, temptingly close to Bronxville and Scarsdale and Greenwich, a portal to the seductive colors of New England and the cool whiteness of a pristine north, even though it is at the same time a mirror of the dull, smoky-skied inner city.

The Bedford Park section of the Bronx, where I grew up, is bounded on the north by Mosholu Parkway; on the south by Fordham Road, the busiest shopping center in the area; on the west by Kingsbridge Heights and Jerome Park; and on the east by Bronx Park and Fordham University. Within those narrow limits there is a good-size city, certainly more than fifty thousand people, as diverse, exhilarating, and threatening as one could expect anywhere.

This northwest corner of the Bronx, part of the Fifty-second Police Precinct, is considered by many to be one of the most dangerous beats in the entire borough. Recently, the *New York Times Magazine* described the area as echoing with random gunfire: "few here are foolish enough to sleep with their bed by a window." The reporter went on, "When the gunmen have a target, as they often do, the next morning the neighbors are out with broom and hose sweeping blood from the sidewalk. All this, of course, creates an air of dread, a feeling best expressed by a T-shirt popular among teenage boys. 'Back up,' it reads, 'and live.'"

The area has the feel of Bombay and Trinidad to it. But it also has something of Korea, Santo Domingo, Puerto Rico, Albania, Vietnam, and particularly from years past there remains a touch of Italy and Ireland. Three hundred police, out of the city's force of thirty thousand uniformed officers, are stationed at the Fifty-second on Webster Avenue. The battle lines have been drawn between hard-working middle-class citizens and the drug pushers and criminals. Sometimes the line is thin, clear as a sheet of plexiglass. So many stores have been robbed repeatedly that often business is conducted from behind such plexiglass partitions. Many people feel that crime in New York City, and particularly in the Bronx, is out of control. With slight shifts, until recently, the number of murders in the city is consistently more than two thousand each year. Three out of every four murders are committed with handguns. More than half a million felonies are committed each year.

The facts suggest that the criminals are winning the war, but in this respect the Bronx, perhaps, is not much different from the rest of the United States, where violence seems to have taken root even in the most rural communities. The Bronx I remembered from the

1960s felt as safe as most small towns are today. Occasionally, we heard of a gang fight and were given an image of the Fordham Baldies carrying chains and knives. It seemed that only professional criminals carried guns—the Mafia, bank robbers, not school children.

The Bronx I knew as a child seemed something like a village. It was encircled by known landmarks. In one direction was the Jerome Park Reservoir. Near the reservoir was a cluster of trees that kept things cool even in the middle of the summer. Harris Field stretched for hundreds of yards in front of the reservoir. We played football and baseball there and softball in the schoolyard of nearby De Witt Clinton High. On the way home after playing we passed alongside the still train yards and then under the IRT elevated subway lines. The rest of my world was limited to the stoops and alleyways to the east along the Grand Concourse, Valentine Avenue, and Bainbridge Avenue down to P.S. 8, where we played basketball or punchball. On the side streets we played stickball, measuring our distances from one manhole cover to another. My southern boundary was 198th Street, the candy store and grocery. Occasionally, I would go the few blocks to Fordham Road, to Alexander's, the movie theaters, the thousands of people and cars, a whirl of strange faces and a chorus of shouts and horns. During the school year my northern limit was St. Philip Neri, but during the summer it contracted to 200th Street and Bedford Park Boulevard, the pizza place, Lew and Artie's soda shop, the deli, the bakery, and the schoolyard behind the Catholic church.

It seemed a defined, safe world. Most of the faces were familiar. None of us would have imagined a drug addict lurking in a shadowy doorway. Violence in school meant a fist fight on the playground. The only time we saw guns they were being carried by cowboys on television, Matt Dillon or Paladin. The Bronx I knew was beginning to disappear long before I left it for good, but something of its small-town atmosphere still remained as I drove away for the last time in the early 1970s. It lingered in some of the faces, in the storefronts, in the occasional sounds of jump ropes scratching against the pavement and Spaldeens popping hollowly off the edge of the sidewalk. It has been about twenty years since I've seen the Bronx. In that time it has made itself, it seems, into myth, a new image of the wasteland, breathtakingly unlivable—dirty, congested, violent—a nightmare symbol that pundits invoke to create a one-word picture of how any American city can de-evolve. As the historian Marshall Berman says in *All That Is Solid Melts into the Air,* the Bronx has become in many minds a code word for our darkest dreams, for our epoch's accumulated horrors: "drugs, gangs, arson, murder, terror, thousands of buildings abandoned, neighborhoods transformed into garbage—and brick—strewn wildernesses."

Some historians of the area look to Robert Moses, the head of the New York City Parks Commission from 1934 to 1960, as the root of the problem in much the same way Mark Twain saw Sir Walter Scott as the destroyer of the South. Among Moses's various duties during his years as an administrator in New York City were responsibility for parks, highways, bridges, slum-clearance projects, and housing developments. His urban ideal was the tower in the park. Most of his architectural projects in New York City were high-rise monoliths, with benches and grassy areas between them. The problem came from their being out of scale, set off from the areas surrounding them. Moses seemed to feel that any house that was old was a slum, no matter how clean or beautiful the house was. Such theories led to low-income projects, the poor quarantined in twenty-story buildings looming over the landscape around them. By the mid-1960s the word *project* had become a synonym for *slum,* and the Bronx became filled with projects.

Moses may have created the central metaphor for places like the Bronx when he built the expressways that reshaped those areas, the morality of the borough becoming the ethic of escape. For some, the expressways were a way out, and for others, a way of believing that things had not changed for the worse. But, as Marshall Berman points out, although many of the avenues seem to recast the old neighborhoods and their virtues—women carrying shopping bags, kids playing ball in the streets, young men conversing on the stoops—what at first glance appears comfortably ordinary is full of darkness: "the nightmare of devastation—a block of burnt-out hulks, a street of rubble and glass where no man goes—surges up in front of us and jars us awake."

Nothing, however, has jarred some historians or some residents into believing that the Bronx is the new wasteland. Some believe that the public impression of the Bronx has always lagged behind the reality. Others say that the "Bronx is burning" syndrome has been snuffed out because new city ordinances and insurance laws have prevented it from being profitable for landlords or tenants to torch their own buildings. Recently, there is more construction going on in the Bronx than in any other part of the city, both reha- bilitation of old buildings and new construction as well. The new buildings are less dense in population than the old apartment buildings were, and even some townhouses are going up.

Another historian of the Bronx, Lloyd Ultan sees the area as vi- brant and alive, charged with people and life, and as safe as anyone could expect an urban area to be in America today. For him, the Bronx is a paragon of peaceful integration in the United States, an urban palette with a beautiful mixture of colors all touching one an- other, closer to an urban ideal than critics would allow and insepa- rable from its past.

The first Europeans to see the Bronx were probably French fur traders in the sixteenth century as they sailed up the Hudson River toward Albany. Perhaps Cabot glimpsed it in 1498 when he saw the lower Hudson, or Verrazano and Gomez might have when they en- tered New York Bay a quarter of a century later.

But whatever Europeans came, three native tribes were there before them—the Rechgawawank, the Wekquaskeck, and the Siwanoy. There were a few settlements, and City Island clam shells were used for wampum, but mainly the area was a hunting ground for the tribes. In 1639 Jonas Bronck, the first European settler, arrived and started a five-hundred-acre plantation of grain and tobacco in the southwest section of the present-day Bronx. Although not much is known about Bronck, he was probably born in Sweden, most likely carried his Lutheran principles to the New World, and was certainly a strong-willed, intelligent Renaissance man. His books were in Latin, Dutch, Danish, and Swedish, and it seems that he taught himself navigation from studying them. But he was more than a scholar, for he accumulated enough money to bring his family and servants to America, where he built a stone house with a tile roof and a large library for his books and some of his eleven woodcuts. He cleared some acreage for his tobacco and animals, horses and cattle, but his pigs ran wild in the woods. Clearly, he was an adventurous man, even an imaginative one—leaving Amsterdam, one of the most stimulating cities in the world at the time, to go into the wilderness to discover a new life. He was also a man of shrewd materialism, and when one of his servant girls, Clara Mathys, married without his permission, he took her husband to court and settled for a sow and a few guilders in reparation for his loss. Bronck died in 1643 at the age of forty-three, leaving behind his name both to the river that coursed through the area and eventually to the borough itself. However, it may have been the early Bronx women who were the most adventurous settlers. Bronck's wife survived him, married again, and after the loss of her second husband in Schenectady she developed her own business, selling guns to the Indian tribes near the Mohawk River. A few years before Bronck died, Anne Hutchinson, mother of fourteen children and the religious reformer who had been excommunicated from the Puritan circle and banished from the Massachusetts Bay Colony for her liberal beliefs, settled in the area near Pelham Bay. Shortly after Bronck's death, she and her family were massacred by the Siwanoy. It was not until more than twenty years later that the first European settlement began in the middle of Westchester.

Slowly, one settlement led to another, and the first federal census in 1790 shows a population of 1,761. Within a century there would be a few hundred thousand people, a number of universities, hospitals, churches, shopping centers, and between the turn of the century and the Great Depression there was an economic boom that led to a population explosion—one million people by 1930. During those years sprouted many of the apartment buildings and neighborhood shopping centers—tailor shops, groceries, hardware and clothing stores.

It is the Bronx of neighborhoods and neighborliness that Lloyd Ultan seems to see as he raises his blue eyes toward the winter clouds in 1993. In front of his apartment near Van Cortlandt Park, he uses his metal cane like a pointer. A professor, Ultan is in his real classroom now. "The Bronx has always been considered a step up the ladder," he says, "but not the final rung. It's a step up from Harlem or the lower East Side. There are certain moves to make— the South Bronx, the Grand Concourse, then Riverdale. Once you are in Riverdale you've made it."

As we drive around my old neighborhood, past the piles of snow blackening to ash, Ultan points out one landmark after another. We pass Fordham University and Poe Cottage, and he lectures on everything from the potato famine and Irish immigration to the writing of "Annabel Lee." The Loew's Paradise looms before us, once a high-ceilinged architectural wonder, a movie theater with a firmament of blinking stars and corridors lined with marble angels, now quadraplexed to fit into the modern world. Past the pierced bell tower of St. Philip Neri Church, its three bells still, frozen in the darkening winter sky. Past Darby's Bog (a slight but significant change from Darby O'Gill's in my day), along Villa Avenue and on to the reservoir in the west. Harris Field, a group of baseball diamonds and football fields, is covered with a few inches of recently fallen snow. A group of teenagers is playing football, slipping and sliding as if they were on a frozen lake.

Ultan is telling me some stories about his books on the Bronx—collections of photographs and essays on the borough in the nineteenth and early twentieth centuries—and recounting anecdotes about Dolores Hope's and E. L. Doctorow's admiration for his work. But my mind has drifted to Harris Field, all the baseball games and all the practices for Pop Warner football that made up my youth. Then I recall my friend Kevin Flynn a quarter of a century ago on that same field.

I was seventeen years old, had been driving for about six months, and Kevin and I had just stepped from my new Pontiac Tempest. With the help of our phony draft cards, we had spent the night in the Inwood Lounge with Dennis Murphy and his brother Michael. About midnight the four of us found ourselves standing in an alcoholic haze in front of the parking meter near my car. The cement around the meter was cracked and crumbling, and the pole was loose in the ground. The night had been uneventful, and with our judgment adrift in cheap scotch we saw the meter as a way of changing that. So, each in turn, we hugged it like a dear, emaciated friend and twisted—until eventually it came free from the sidewalk.

We dumped it into the trunk like a dead body and sped off laughing. Back at Bedford Park Boulevard and Jerome Avenue we parked the car, the Murphys wisely excused themselves, and Kevin and I discussed what we should do with our prize. We decided to carry it to Harris Field, surely deserted at that time of night, and crack the head of the meter open to split the change, which, as I recall the shallow jingling sound, would probably have netted us about $1.80. But after we had come this far, it seemed our duty to see the adventure to the end.

We carried the meter between us, me at the head, Kevin at the cement-knobbed base of the pole, an old jacket draped over it, for what reason I can't now recall. We headed west, past the Bedford Park train station, where a transit officer observed us from behind the door. I knew he saw us and must have wondered if we carried some skinny, misshapen body to be tossed into the reservoir, but we didn't turn back, just quickened our pace.

At Harris Field we ran up the slope and took turns cracking the meter against the cement. Either the cracks shattering the night silence or the transit officer alerted the police, and I saw the flashing lights as I held the meter raised in the air, my feet apart, as if I were some early Bronx settler getting ready to split a piece of firewood. I let it drop, saying, "Let's get the hell out of here!"

Kevin was already running through the open gate onto the field. It was a few hundred yards from one side of the field to the other gate. Maybe we thought we could outrun a couple of potbellied New York City cops. Maybe we didn't think. I caught up with Kevin and was a few yards ahead of him when I realized with sickening suddenness that there were lights flashing behind us, that the police car had driven up the slope and was coming across the field. Every ounce of alcohol had been burnt off by adrenaline, and I was thinking with a quick, pulsing clarity. I tried to calculate how many yards we had to go to get to the pedestrian gate, the gate that would force the police car to stop. I tried to determine how fast the car was speeding toward us. I imagined being run over, scoured into the summer grass, an absurd trench for tomorrow's baseball players to ponder quizzically. Oddly enough, given my terror, George Orwell's story "Shooting an Elephant," which I had recently read in school, burst into my mind with the image of the Dravidian coolie, lying on his belly, the skin stripped from his back, arms crucified, head twisted sharply to one side, teeth bared and grinning, . . . but it was my face. We didn't stop, just ran faster, the alcohol and sweat flying from us like exhaust fumes.

We beat the car to the gate by a second or two and flew down the slope on the other side. Running full speed, hearing the police car doors slam behind me, I yelled to Kevin, "Hide!" The breath that propelled the one syllable, because I couldn't have managed more, also seemed to help me dive forward in midrun and land, shirt torn, patches of skin ripped from my hands and arms, under a parked *New York Daily News* truck. I lay there for a moment, my heart beating so loudly I was certain it would give away my hiding spot, and listened to the footsteps race by me. Then I heard: "Stop or I'll shoot!" With that I was certain Kevin would be killed, and I would spend years in prison for some complicated federal offense—laying hands on a parking meter, somehow akin to manslaughter or sexual assault. I saw myself transformed in a moment, as Rip had been. I had entered the night as myself, but sunrise would find me aged twenty years—a man, a convict, no longer a boy.

I lay there for seconds, then minutes, and there was no shot, just an expanding silence. I crawled out from under the truck, looked around into the darkness for Kevin, and headed for home to wait for the FBI to knock on the door: "You're under arrest. Kevin Flynn ratted on you." It was only fair that he would, and I waited next to the phone until three in the morning, when the first ring caught my eyelids drooping into sleep.

Kevin was safe at home, and no arrests would be made. Kevin had been caught, and the police marched him back to the vicinity where they had first seen us, but with his Irish instinct for storytelling and his steely nerves he told them, an apologetic look in his green eyes, that we were under age, drinking, and were afraid to get caught. According to Kevin, one of the officers did a quick search for the abandoned liquor, stumbled over the parking meter in the darkness as Kevin's heart missed a beat, and told him to get home before he took him down to the station house.

Ultan's laugh brings me back to the present. He cocks his head, looks over at me: "So Dolores Hope slaps me on the shoulder and says, 'You, you, I just had to buy all of your books.' " His laugh drifts behind us as we pass a crowd of Asian students coming from the Bronx High School of Science. We circle back toward his apartment, and I note the names of some of the stores—Caribbean Choice Bakery, Salgado Food Market, Indian Food, Battembay Market, Home Boy 200. In the sea of new names, the Jolly Tinker is a familiar one on Webster Avenue. The graffiti, the razor-edged barbed wire, the music thumping nervously from the storefronts are all new, but it's the past I hear now most clearly, Kevin's voice and Murphy's and the sound of our footsteps as we ran from a new Bronx that seemed crafted by "the industrious hand of man."

When I grew up in New York City, we used the term *BIC*, Bronx Irish Catholic, derisively. For us, it meant girls in plaid skirts and saddle shoes, boys in Oxford shirts and khaki pants. It meant the smiling Kingston Trio and a happy acceptance of the way the world was. So even though most of us were BICs, we pictured ourselves otherwise. Perhaps this is always the story of boyhood, a story that in many ways is ever the same, about the desperate attempt to disappear and reappear transformed, but also about regretting what has been left behind, a tale told in fragments, the way the past seems to us, epiphanic moments, luminous or grotesque, a circle rather than a straight line. It is a story of anticipation. In a sense, in the Bronx we were all like Rip, listening carefully to hear the sound of our new names, whatever they would be, and waiting to see where our new selves would lead us, for I'm certain we all assumed that the Bronx was a place to start from and not a place to end up.

CHAPTER 1
················

Lot's Wife *and*
Other Bronx Women

Remember Lot's Wife.

—Luke, 17:32

First of all, she had a name, and she had a history.
—Scott Cairns,
"The Turning of Lot's wife"

From what I have seen, I am driven to the conclusion that religion is only good for good people, and I do not mean this as a paradox, but simply as an observable fact. Only good people can afford to be religious. For the others, it is too great a temptation—a temptation to the deadly sins of pride and anger, chiefly, but one might also add sloth.
—Mary McCarthy,
Memories of a Catholic Girlhood

I was born shortly before the Soviets exploded their first atomic bomb—pushed into a new world, placed on the edge of a cold war shadowed by nuclear clouds. A few years later, Joseph McCarthy, the demagogic senator from Wisconsin, branded his name upon the

25

decade, a dark time full of cowardice and shame, lonely bravery and martyrdom.

By the time I started the first grade at St. Philip Neri Elementary School in 1955, McCarthy had already been censured by the Senate. Soon after, the American press began to ignore him. He was dead before I got far enough along in school to even learn who he was and what he had left behind. But as I look back on my early years in school, I now see that some of those Ursuline nuns must have learned a great deal from McCarthy's tactics, as he must have learned from their masters, the judges in the Inquisition.

On my first day of school I got lost and I met Benny Ianello, two bad signs for the future. My mother had walked me to 200th Street and the Grand Concourse, a few hundred yards from the school. She had left me there, thinking, I believe, that it would be better for me to begin negotiating such journeys on my own. Certainly she was right, and how was she to know that all those winding lines of boys and girls and all those nuns, their habits skittering in the wind like frightened black birds, would make me suspect that I would never return to my old life? I looked over my shoulder as I headed toward the school, and I saw my mother, her dark hair dancing in the breeze, turn back to wave. The scent of her perfume, along with her smile, flew back to me, and I moved forward.

Students were lined up in front of the church, which was next to the school building. I couldn't find my class and began to cry, but I was soon noticed by Benny Ianello, who graciously sought assistance for me by tugging on a nun's sleeve and saying, "That baby over there is crying because he's lost." She directed me to the end of the same line Benny was in, and when she walked away, he turned around and smiled, his black eyebrows arching. His knowing grin stopped my tears immediately and made me realize this was the first lesson school had to teach me.

My next important lesson came from Mother Concepta, one of my teachers, but Benny Ianello had a hand in that one too. Mother Concepta was small and frail. Her wrists, beneath the billowing black cotton sleeves that enveloped them, looked dry and brittle. Wire-rimmed glasses, balanced on the thin bridge of her nose, were partly hidden by the bandeau, a starched piece of white cloth that attached to a chin band. She was sharp and definite in all of the scant angles of flesh exposed—her cheekbones and fingers mainly. Layers of cotton and silk and wool—veils and mantles and scapulars—made her seem wraithlike. Her habit left little more than a pencil line of mouth and eyes that seemed to be chips of basalt. The rest of her was a ghostly mystery. She floated along in those first months of school in her long black robe, pushed by breezes that barely moved the crucifix hanging from her neck. She had left us in the classroom, telling us to work silently. But the dark-skinned Benny had poked me, which led to a duel, Saracen against Crusader, our pencils flashing like sabers.

I didn't notice her when she came back into the room, but I heard the sound the rosary made, beads clicking against the small cross, as she returned. I looked up and then down again at the blood pooling up in the palm of my right hand. In the center of the bright red circle was an eye of graphite left by the pencil. She looked at me evenly, without anger, took my right hand in hers, a plain gold band on her finger glinting in the classroom lights, and asked, "How did this happen?" I lied, of course, explaining that Benny had asked me a question, and I had turned around, my hand accidentally speared by his extended pencil. I wasn't protecting Benny, but myself. I would have been happy to see him punished, for I hadn't fully forgotten the first day of school.

She didn't say another word until she got me to the nurse's office. At first we both stared at my extended palm and the wound that bubbled up like a bloodshot eye. We watched the trickle of blood pool into the lifeline and make a slim stream toward my index finger. Then she questioned my story from all angles.

"Mr. Pearson, *why* did you turn around?"

"Because Benny asked me a question."

"And what was the question?"

"Uh, he wanted to know about Lent, when it started."

"More than three months away. But he wanted to know now?"

"Well, I guess he was thinking about what to give up."

"Do you know what God does to children who lie, Mr. Pearson, to those who disobey?"

"Yes, sister, I know."

I had only a vague idea, but I was willing to take my chances on the unknown rather than submit to the everyday kind of punishment that I had witnessed for months. I held fast to the lie, and finally she relented. Or so I thought at first. The next day she took away my honor roll pin. Talking when she was out of the room, she said. On Monday of the following week, before our work began, she told us the story of Lot's wife:

"Sodom and Gomorrah were evil places, children. Two messengers were sent by God to destroy the cities and the sinners who lived in them. At the entrance to the cities, the angels of God met Lot, who was kind to them, as he always was to strangers. For his generosity God decided to spare him and his family, giving them a chance to escape. Lot tried to convince his friends and his sons-in-law to leave with him before God destroyed the towns, but everyone laughed at him.

"Finally, Lot left without them, escaping with his wife and two daughters. 'Flee for your lives,' the angels said. 'Don't look back, and don't stop anywhere along the plain. Don't stop until you reach the mountains, or you will be swept away by the wrath of God.' "

Here Mother Concepta canted her head a bit more in my direction before continuing. I glanced away from her shifting eyes, out the classroom window, at the Grand Concourse, which for me at that moment was the only highway through the Bronx, the only one I knew that led out of the Bronx.

"Lot and his family left, and God rained down fire and brimstone on the wicked cities, destroying everyone and everything there. Lot's family ran from the flames and the screams, but Lot's wife did not obey."

At this point Mother Concepta looked directly at me.

"Lot's wife turned around. She looked back. She disobeyed, boys and girls. And God turned her into a pillar of salt. Remember Lot's wife, children. Remember her."

At least once a week for the rest of the year Mother Concepta told the story, working the drama exactly the same way each time, using her eyes like the lens of a camera, sweeping wide until she came to her salty moral: then a closeup on me.

After hearing the story of Lot's wife half a dozen times or so, I began to get lost in the hum of the words themselves, in the rasping repetition of her voice. I began to forget Lot's wife and to wonder about Mother Concepta. What was hidden beneath her habit—a shaved head, a flat chest, a sexless cartoon being? All of us, boys and girls, I'm certain, spent many hours during those elementary school years contemplating the mysterious physiognomy of nuns. What sort of creatures were they? What did they eat? What did they do at night? How did they sleep in those black gowns, for we couldn't imagine them unrobed, in dresses or jeans or, God forbid, T-shirts.

Those questions, of course, were never answered, and by the time we were old enough to realize that they were women, like other women, we were too old to be stunned by such a revelation. The mystery of the sisterhood didn't seem important by that time. But the story of Lot's wife stayed with me, and I wondered occasionally during those elementary school years why that story angered me so much. It wasn't merely disgust at being caught in a lie or annoyance over being singled out. By the time I reached high school, I figured out what bothered me about the story. I read the tale and discovered that Lot wasn't all that admirable. When the Sodomites came angrily to his door, seeking to harm the strangers who were his guests, Lot very unselfishly offered his daughters instead: "No, my friends, do not be so wicked. Look, I have two daughters, both virgins; let me bring them out to you, and you can do what you like with them." *But* he didn't offer himself. However, it wasn't Lot's cowardly generosity, his wormy religious correctness, or the fact that later on he was so easily tricked into sleeping with his two daughters that bothered me the most. I simply couldn't view Lot's wife as the villain. I couldn't see her looking back at the devastation and death as wrong. For me, it suggested that she could not easily turn away from the past. Her imagination, her curiosity, and her inability to shut out human suffering forced her to disobey even the most powerful rules. The way I saw it, Lot ended up cursed in his flesh, but his wife ended up a monument.

Of course, I encountered many nuns besides Mother Concepta during eight years in elementary school. Most of them were calm and loving, many had a gentle sense of humor, but other than Mother Concepta's, it is the face of Mother David that I can still see.

Mother David looked like a grim version of Willa Cather, blunt featured and masculine and with none of the angelic softness the writer had about her eyes and mouth. Mother David's eyes were points of steel, and she spoke in the clipped rhythms of a street fighter rather than in the clear poetry of Cather's narratives. There was something fierce and brutal about her. Like Mother Concepta, she believed in silent obedience and swift punishment for any defiance of authority, but unlike Mother Concepta, she had little sense of subtlety.

We were in the fifth grade, and she would be our last woman teacher in elementary school. After fourth grade, girls and boys were placed in separate classes, actually placed in separate parts of the building. Some theory about patent leather shoes, plaid skirts, sperm cells, friction, and the occasion of sin was behind it all, but I never got much further than contemplating the mysteries of what, after all, patent leather shoes might explain to me. Most of us merely accepted such segregations as part of growing up. For a time after fourth grade, girls became just another mystery like the Holy Trinity.

Perhaps it was merely coincidence that Mother David was more manly than the male teachers we were about to have from the next year forward, but it seemed a part of a larger plan to have her lead us toward the brothers, the paddlings, and the more masculine cruelties that lay ahead. The year with her was one of barked commands snapping us to attention. It was more like boot camp than grade school, but that made sense at the time because a few months before, in our bloodred robes, we had been confirmed, slapped by the bishop, made soldiers of Christ.

By the middle of the year most of us knew how to survive in Mother David's class, but Billy Donnelly had just moved into the neighborhood and had only been in our class for a week. We knew enough not to make eye contact when she had caught us in some misdemeanor, but Billy was too new, his antenna not refined enough to pick up certain signals.

Whatever he had done wrong, Billy made things worse by not looking abjectly down when Mother David called his name. Instead, he looked directly at her, uncowed and unremorseful. She strode down to his seat in the middle of the room. Heads shifted for a better view.

"Mr. Donnelly, hold out your hand."

"But Sister . . ." he began.

"Mr. Donnelly, hold out your hand." She said it slowly, as if she were speaking a foreign language.

A weak, forced smile crept into the corners of his mouth, the edges of his eyes. He held his hand out, palm up. Mother David lifted a thick ruler from the seemingly endless black folds of her habit. It appeared to be a magician's trick, and for a moment I expected a string of handkerchiefs, a rabbit, a gold doubloon. But the trick stopped with the wooden ruler. She reached back and struck his hand, producing a sound that made most of us flinch in pain and surprise. It was the sound that took us off guard, a sharper crack than it seemed possible for flesh to create. She raised her hand again, but this time the ruler cut through air and silence. Billy had moved his hand, almost in the way a child will in a game of slap hands, but his movement had a visceral desperation to it, unplanned, as if the hand had a mind of its own. The silence spread out like spilled water, and we waited to see what Mother David would do or say. I'm certain that none of us came close to guessing what she would do. She didn't hit him again or send him to the principal. She just looked down as if she had tasted something sour, opened her lips to spit it out, and snapped, "Chicken!" Then she walked back to the front of the classroom without looking at Billy again and continued her lesson. I had heard boys call each other *chicken* many times, but I had never heard a nun say it. From her, it sounded like an obscenity.

Mother David was tough, and she believed in retribution, but compared with the iron-haired Mrs. Murther, our penmanship teacher, she was a source of infinite compassion and understanding. Mrs. Murther did not tolerate mistakes. As I remember her, she was always dressed in some dull shade of pink, but no color could soften her dour disposition. She was heavy, and she acted like a weight on everything around her. When she walked into the classroom, the very air became leaden with a crabbed gravity. She never once smiled as she taught the Palmer Method, chastising us if we didn't make fluid, looping circles, our pencils flowing cursively across wide-ruled paper. I imagined my hand as a hawk gliding along on the wind currents between the lines, between heaven and earth. But I concentrated too hard at times, perhaps, on keeping my hand straight as if I were balancing weightless pennies on the top of it. When the ache rose from my fingers into my forearm and shoulder, I lost the image of the hawk and thought of myself as a soldier—*keep your hand straight,* I'd tell myself . . . *neatness, order, control.* The result, though, was not calligraphy. It wasn't crimped or illegible. It was just ordinary.

Not being able to make my Ms and Ws splash into one another like waves upon a shore made me love words more, not less, for they took on a certain mystery and, because of Mrs. Murther, a thrilling sense of danger. That is, it was dangerous to make a mistake in her class, especially if you were using a fountain pen—the nib slipping, the ink pooling up like an oil spill at the base of an L or G, or the cartridge somehow self-destructing. Then we had blue hands or tongues, smeared pages, blurred letters, and Mrs. Murther's calculated fury.

Worse than the page was the blackboard. It was Mrs. Murther's domain. Many students stayed home on Wednesdays, penmanship day, with stomach pains, earaches, dizziness, odd tremors, or any exotic disease that might not insult the ordinary good sense of a parent. Those who attended school on that day came for one of two reasons—either they had run out of excuses, or they were sanguine by nature, believing it possible that Mrs. Murther had died of a heart attack the night before. These students would try to squeeze themselves into invisibility by sheer willpower as she started to call people to the board to show their mastery of upstrokes, horizontal lines, and ligatures.

We all knew what would happen if the letters were stiff, too small, or slanted in the wrong direction. Mrs. Murther would first make the writer face the class, his letters behind him like a verdict.

She would explain the mistake, wondering aloud about the lack of practice, the laziness, that could be behind such ineptness. Then she would take a handful of the student's hair and bang his head neatly and matter-of-factly three times against the blackboard, sharp cracks of bone against slate. There never seemed to be any spontaneous anger. Always the same three smacks. Always the same icy smile. Most of us would silently walk back to our seats, a bit dazed and dry-eyed as the chalk dust settled to the floor like radioactive particles. Mrs. Murther would return to the blackboard, never turning to watch the student drag himself back to his seat. Then she would erase the offending script and put a new sentence on the board. Our penmanship did not improve, nor did our love for critics swell, but we probably all sensed that no criticism of our writing after that could be quite as blunt or embarrassing.

The Bronx, as I remember it then, was filled with the faces of women. They looked down from the fourth-floor windows of apartment buildings, their arms resting on the dusty sills as their children called up to them, asking for a quarter or if they could go to the schoolyard to play. Those women came in all sizes and shapes. They were round and square. They had the faces of sad-eyed horses and porcelain angels. Their hair was raven and red. Their voices were pleasant whispers or loud commands that could stop a boy cold in his tracks two blocks away in the heat of summer.

Molly Grossman, who lived in my apartment building down the hall by the mailboxes, would always remind us to wear any new outfit "in good health." For us, she was never Mrs. Grossman, always Molly, squat and smiling, her words rolling into our ears with a pleasant, tickling accent: "So, vat's the madder?" It wasn't until I was about to begin college that I realized her story was the immigrant's tale in the United States, a story of escape and courage and strength of character. She was one of the thousands of Anne Franks who had survived to tell their stories in the plain language of daily existence in the days and months of their lives in new countries. She had come to America as a young girl, filled with hope but surely aware of how hard the world could be, and had contentedly made her slow progress into the lower middle class, by increments had found her way into the northern Bronx. She worked as a seamstress in a dress factory and met a serious, angular young man who was a waiter in a restaurant in midtown Manhattan. Soon after, they got married, they had two children, and he turned fleshy and jocular. He became the kind of man that all children wanted to address as *grandfather*, even before he was middle-aged. After he died, Molly became an adopted grandmother to my sister and me.

Her apartment was at the dark far end of the first-floor corridor. Her back window looked onto the farthest part of the alleyway and the weed-strewn, rock-littered yards of the two-family houses that stood on the northern end of Valentine Avenue. Occasionally, I saw her wheeling a laundry cart or grocery basket up the street, but most of my meetings with her were in the half-lit hallway. She would sit down with me on the bench near the mailboxes and ask me about what I was learning in school. In the dim light of the hallway I would look at her, imagining she was my grandmother who came from another world, a Polish Jew with an exotic accent. "Vait a minute," she would always say and then disappear into her apartment, bringing out a piece of hard candy. "Here, you're such a good boy. I think you might become president some day." If my mother were not home, my sister and I would go to Molly's apartment. When my mother was sick in the hospital, Molly gave us dinner, making my sister giggle beneath her open hand when Molly gently scolded, "Get away from the wreng, children," as she pointed at the stove.

She was always there if we rang her bell, as if she were waiting for us. We took it for granted that she had always been there, always would be. Other women in the building—Mrs. Coyle, Mrs.

Moody, Mrs. Conley, Mrs. Bornaman—had their own children. Molly's Grace and Sam were grown. That left Molly for us. Often I would sit in the entranceway between the kitchen and the bathroom in our apartment, playing with toy cowboys and Indians, listening to the rise and swell of the conversation between my mother and Molly at the kitchen table, like mother and grandmother exchanging stories.

Molly was the other side of Mrs. Murther and Mother David, but just as they were, she *was* the Bronx. It is hard to imagine that time and place without her or them. Molly's eyes were always fixed on the people and objects around her, not anxiously searching the distances.

Molly reminded me of Mrs. Murphy, my friend Dennis's mother. Mrs. Murphy never failed to offer a cup of tea, no matter how wilting the humidity. When we thought of Mrs. Murphy, "Cup o' tea, boys?" became like a punch line to a standing joke. She always wore a floral print housedress that rippled like a Bedouin tent as she waddled through the rooms of her apartment. Her stockings were always bunched around her fleshy knees. She also wore the same round-faced look of bemusement each time she spoke to us, a gleam in her eye that implied she was entertained by our foolishness, by the strangeness of life itself. Like Molly, Mrs. Murphy had come to this new world as a young woman, alone but unblinking in the face of what lay ahead of her. What lay ahead was a simple, ordinary life—cleaning other people's homes, riding the subway each evening, raising her two sons, whom she was certain had kissed the Blarney stone too many times for their own good.

But then there was Mrs. Barcai, skeletal and unsmiling, who wore her mid-European Jewishness like a dark cloak. She was our landlady at 2902 Grand Concourse; her apartment was on the second floor, and on only two occasions in the twenty-one years I lived there did I see her outside it. My mother would often ask me to take the rent money to her, and I would stand in the dark hallway, ring the bell, and wait for her to look through the peephole before cracking the door open and glumly taking the check from my outstretched hand. She was a widow, and I never saw any children visit her. It was as if something she had run from in Europe still haunted her, had followed her to this new country.

As a child, I associated these women with their apartments. The sound of their voices—Jewish, Italian, Irish accents—rose and fell in the various rooms. Their faces in the summertime were framed by the open windows as they leaned their arms on the fire escapes and talked to a neighbor on the street below. I saw these women in the kitchens, smelling of tomato sauce and corned beef. Without them, the apartments would have been faceless, odorless, silent, still as tombs.

Our apartment building was like many others in the Bronx. It had five stories and four apartments on each floor. In those twenty apartments we lived our lives a few feet from each other without ever knowing very much about how our individual stories might converge. The layout of our one-bedroom apartment was much like many of the others in the building. A solid metal door opened to face the living room. A narrow hallway led left to a small bathroom and right to the kitchen, which contained a dining table squeezed against the window and a food cabinet by the sink. In the cabinet, the cereal and canned goods filled the shelves above my father's tools. I associated that cabinet with Wheaties and screwdrivers, the smell of graham crackers and Three-in-One oil, but also with cockroaches. If I came out after bedtime and pulled the string to the kitchen light, the cockroaches were there in the closet, sometimes in the sink, their crisp shells scraping against porcelain or wood as they scurried from the light. The living room had a steam pipe rising up from the floor and going through the ceiling to the apartment above ours. Next to the steam pipe was the radiator, on which my sister and I always sat for a few moments after coming in from playing in the cold. The windows behind the hissing radiator looked out onto the back alley and the two-family houses on Valentine Avenue. The bedroom was off to the right of the living room. It had two beds, a dresser, and the one closet in the apartment. The bedroom window faced the street, the Grand Concourse, which probably was once grand, with elegant ladies and gentlemen promenading along it, but at bedtime to me it seemed merely wide and filled with the rattling sounds of subways and the monotonous roar of city buses.

When my father stopped at the bar after work at a construction site, he brought home with him a history of disappointments and frustrations. On those evenings, and there were many of them, the apartment was too small for all the bad feeling that came with him. His whiskey voice filled up the rooms. There was no place to escape it.

When my sister and I were alone with my mother, the apartment seemed spacious. We felt free to move about and speak our minds. My mother's smile had a steady, unflickering warmth, which sometimes would be enough to protect us even against cold stares, accusations, and hard silences.

Other families in other apartments—the Conleys, the Moodys, the Hanleys—lived lives much like ours, I assumed. The fathers worked with their scarred hands, they drank, they carried dark secrets. I knew that Richie Conley's life, like mine, was tidal, and Durella's Bar was the moon. Richie, too, was drawn back and forth by his father's moods, his life awash in his father's drinking, in the shadow of his anger.

Nearly always, it was the women, not the men, who were able to leave the apartments and come into the light, who brought talk into the open. The women gossiped on the front steps, talked on the lines at Drewsen's Delicatessen or Haecker's Bakery, and exchanged pleasantries as they wheeled their laundry carts around the corner. They strolled home from the market together—those metal laundry carts sometimes doing double duty as shopping baskets, rolling tipsily behind them filled with paper sacks of food— and talked about the butcher, the baker, and their husbands. These women smelled of laundry detergent, fresh bread, and peaches in the summertime and of chopped meat, onions, and ground coffee in the winter. Their eyes were soft and understanding. There were exceptions, of course—women like Mrs. Barcai or Mrs. Wall, the superintendent of our apartment building. Mrs. Wall had an icy Slavic seriousness that never melted. She lived at the end of the long tunnel in the basement apartment, amidst the garbage cans and the coal dust. If we played in that tunnel or the alcove that led to the dumb waiter, she would make a guttural sound, chase us away with a broom, and return without a backward glance to her life underground.

Most of the women I remember in the Bronx, however, like I imagined Lot's wife, seemed always ready to look back with concern and compassion. Mrs. Kane said how handsome we were becoming; Mrs. Hanley always asked about school; Sarah, the candy store owner, slipped free pieces of gum or chocolate into our hands as we left her place. Letty and Loretta, who lived in the more elegant apartments in the next building, we called aunts even though there was no family connection.

The apartment building where Letty and Loretta lived, 2910 Grand Concourse, was adjacent to the fenced-in gardens that separated it from the Susan Devin building, a residence hall for nuns, for me a mysterious place with a common dining room and shuttered windows. I passed the building each day with a backward glance into the shuttered spaces. I always stopped to peer through the bars of the fence into the Italianate garden, a plot of ground that could have been imagined by Hawthorne. The garden was always still, empty except for a sparrow or butterfly, and the hallways were always silent. Occasionally, I would see a dark-haired old man, with a hook nose and a hawkish profile, bent in the wind, at work in the garden with a spade or a shovel. But I never saw anyone enjoying the garden area. I never saw any picnics or heard any laughter. So it always seemed to me more of an artifact than a place, as if it were somehow a decoration attached to the pale bricks of 2910 Grand Concourse. It could have been Rappaccini's garden, beautiful and poisonous.

Both Letty and Loretta seemed suited to their building. Even though it was attached to my apartment building, theirs seemed a world apart, more elegant, meant for a separate class of people. It was a reminder of a time when the Bronx may have considered itself a country retreat from the city, a time when couples promenaded up and down the Grand Concourse. They were spinster aunts, not wives or nuns. Rather, they were something undefined. Letty could be cool and at times show a Gaelic sarcasm, but her tone was never sharp enough to change the soft-fleshed roundness of her face or to alter the careful attentiveness of her eyes. Loretta was fragile looking, her skin stretched like warm glass over her bones. She reminded me of a Kansas schoolmarm, thin and plain. She was reserved but not cold—more, it seemed, unworldly. I always expected her neck to be covered by a high lace collar as if she were a Victorian dame. She lived in a different era—right next door to me. Her building was everything mine was not. It had a buzzer that allowed visitors to enter the mirrored, carpeted lobby, an open area with soft lights and sofas, and, unlike any of the buildings I knew in the Bronx, it had an elevator as well. Letty and Loretta lived together in an apartment whose windows overlooked the Susan Devin garden. They entertained guests in a sunken living room, two steps below the main section of the apartment. Apparently, theirs was a world without men—placid, consistent, gentle.

Although I grew up hearing stories about the storms of their pasts—lost loves, young men stricken by exotic diseases—these two women seemed to live quietly with their memories in the present. When I spoke to them, their eyes, like fixed points in a midnight sky, stayed focused on me.

In the center of my world in the Bronx was my own mother. Her eyes always seemed to shine with good humor, and never, as far as I can remember, did she raise her voice in anger. Mostly, my sister and I did exactly what she said, partly out of love and partly out of a protective instinct. My father could disrupt our lives at any moment. Our disobedience would have placed her in jeopardy, and neither of us wanted that. My mother seemed soft and yielding, and maybe my sister and I thought she was vulnerable enough already without our adding to the hazard. Often she embarrassed us when we were children by asking too many questions of waiters, tour guides, or bus drivers. We were used to men's silences, unasked questions sizzling like lit fuses. As we got older, we grew to admire her innocence, her love of the world around her, her courage, her quick excitement. We recognized then, I believe, that her softness was actually a strength, an unyielding faith in possibilities. What I recall most vividly about her is a habit of attentiveness—simply that, like Loretta and Molly, she looked at us when we spoke, and she listened. She always listened.

Her habit of listening was a natural part of her hopefulness, I think, a quiet sense of optimism. She believed that stories could change a person's life, so she paid attention to people and their stories. To stories in general. In a house and in a culture that seemed aware of only newsprint, she loved books. My father read the newspaper every week night and every morning on weekends at the kitchen table, the ink barely visible on his weathered fingers. While he read about a murder on Mott Street, she read Dostoevsky. She would sit on the living room sofa, a small brown bag of various-colored hard candy by her side and a book opened in her lap. My father's eyes were always hidden behind the *Daily News,* which he held up like a screen. My mother's eyes were always visible, a gaze that could rise at any moment as she described some part of the story she read. For her, books were just an extension of the world, an entryway to secret places. Her own story was undramatic, she thought, and not worth telling in one continuous narrative, so the details came out in bits and pieces over the years.

She had grown up in the lower Bronx at 574 East 156th Street, the cross of St. Jerome's Church rising into view from her apartment window. Her mother, Genevieve, whom everyone called Jennie, was a Findlan, but she was brought up by an aunt and uncle and called herself an O'Pray. She married a man named Christopher Fluhr, had three sons, and when he died, married Alfred Hunter, my mother's father, a dark-haired, fastidious man who had his stepsons polish his boots each morning before he stepped out the door. Hunter had emigrated from somewhere in the north of Ireland—perhaps from Belfast or Londonderry, a textile worker or a shopkeeper. Or maybe he had been unemployed and encouraged by the damp winds off the North Channel in Ballycastle to seek his fortune in New York City. Whatever his reasons for leaving Ireland, Hunter barely stayed around long enough in the city to see his child, and then he went away, back to Northern Ireland or into a windblown anonymity in Chicago. He was gone, as if he had become bored with his part in the plot he had created. He went out, possibly, to find another story to live. His name was never mentioned after he left. It was as if he never existed. And, many years later, by the time any questions arose again about him, no one seemed sure where he came from or where he escaped to; he was not a memory, but a figure in a dream.

My own mother grew up, shy and sheltered, protected by older brothers, her mother, and her Aunt Carrie, so protected that she

knew practically nothing about her real father until a few years before she got married after World War II when she was in her
midthirties. Her brother Walter died when he was nineteen years
old. He was in the hospital to have a carbuncle treated and expected to be kept overnight. The next morning, when his mother
came to pick him up, he was dying from blood poisoning. She came
into the room, and he turned to her with a look of surprise before
his eyes lost focus and he died. My mother was five years old then.
Her brother Bob, perhaps feeling that the world could not be
trusted, watched over her more carefully, not wanting anyone in his
family to be taken by surprise again. Her other brother, Vincent,
had the looks of a silent film star, and he played the piano with the
same cruel economy that he used with people. He came to enjoy
hurting his friends and family, watching their stunned faces as if he
took pleasure in knowing that he could not be caught off guard by a
malicious fate if he were mean enough himself. He faded into the
Midwest, lost like his stepfather, escaping other people's stories
and hiding his own.

My mother grew up calling herself Fluhr after the man who
had died years before she was born. When she was born, in 1911,
the Bronx still had trolley cars and a scattering of farms. Many of
the roads were dirt, and it was not all that unusual to see cows dot-
ting a hillside. The Grand Concourse had just been completed.
Only its side roads were paved. Its center was a turf track for horses
and carriages. But this world into which she was born—a year after
the return of Halley's comet and Mark Twain's death, the year before the sinking of the *Titanic*—transformed itself before her eyes
like a magic trick, buildings rising out of nowhere, roads hardening
into ribbons of asphalt, trolleys vanishing, and cars and buses taking their place.

She graduated from Cathedral High School and went straight
into the Great Depression, but she hardly felt its consequences

while she lived at home and had a salary of $12.50 a week. One year she took courses in philosophy and poetry at the Manhattan branch of Fordham University. There, for the first time, she fell under the spell of books, another set of voices to listen to, of characters to know, of stories to lead her back into the world while at the same time holding it at bay.

When my mother was twenty-four years old, her mother died of an embolism. My mother was going by train for a vacation in Pennsylvania, and she remembers her mother's sad expression, as if she knew that would be their last conversation. The next day, in Pennsylvania, my mother got the news from her brother Bob, but even then, protective, he didn't tell her the truth, just that she should come home to care for her mother.

Then she was alone, carrying a jumble of names—O'Pray, Fluhr, Hunter, Findlan—and within a few years she met my father, a handsome sailor, and took one more name, this one Anglicized, invented for the world, but finally offering her no more protection than Hunter had. At first, their one-bedroom apartment had been filled with the sound of guitar strings and the smell of potato pancakes and pickled beets. But within a few years the living room grew silent, and in the kitchen the hum of the refrigerator made the silence audible. Beer cans began to fill the garbage bag, and my father's plate sat at his place, untouched. By the time my sister and I were school age, we ate most of our dinners without my father, who usually lingered at one of the neighborhood bars before coming home. We would eat our lamb chops, or our pot roast and noodles, or our fish sticks on Fridays during Lent, answer my mother's questions, and tell her the stories of our day at St. Philip Neri. I'd lean my elbows on the cool formica table and listen to my sister talk of Mother Annunciata and Cathy Cunningham. If we finished dinner, we would be reading in the living room when he came home, and our books and magazines, in a way, protected us. They gave us a place for our gaze and allowed another voice inside our heads.

If the door lock clicked before we were finished with dinner, the food turned hard and cold in my stomach, and there was no place to escape. My father would stumble against the kitchen closet and look at the three of us as if he had caught us in a shameful act.

"Sit down, Gus, I'll get you a plate," my mother would say, her voice sounding unfamiliar, like someone I didn't know.

"I don't want any of this crap," he'd reply and stare at us until we all looked down at our plates. And we'd wait. Wait for it to be over, for him, finally, to bang the bedroom door shut.

This happened over and over again, and although throughout those years there was some talk of leaving and even a mention of divorce once or twice, my mother never budged. Her reasons for staying were never fully clear to my sister and me, and probably not to my mother either. It may have had something to do with the picture of a family that had been placed in her mind years before. Or it may have been that, without a father herself, she didn't want us to lose ours. It may have been Catholicism or just her belief that her own words and stories would fill the void that gaped wider every day. Somehow she learned how to survive with whatever power innocence could give her in a world that often seemed shaped by anger and despair.

On the day after President Kennedy was assassinated, my mother took me to Madison Square Garden on Fiftieth Street and Eighth Avenue to see the Knicks play the Detroit Pistons. She had taken me to a few games the year before, when I was in the eighth grade, and I dreamt of Richie Guerin, the stellar New York guard who averaged nearly thirty points per game during the 1962 season, as I lay in bed planning my own moves on the St. Philip Neri basketball squad.

My mother seemed to enjoy different things about the game than I did. She nodded politely as I explained what "traveling" meant or why a certain foul had been called. Richie Guerin was my hero, with his two-hand set shot and lightning quick drive to the basket. My mother adored Tom Stith, the rookie, who always blessed himself at the foul line.

That Saturday night, even though games had been canceled in Boston and Los Angeles, the New York owners decided to have the Knicks play. I'm not sure now why we even decided to go to the game. Perhaps, as many others did during those days, we moved like sleepwalkers through our appointments and daily routines. The city appeared to be in a trance. The eyes of the subway riders were more glazed than usual. The dinner crowd at Mama Leone's was subdued. There was no music and little laughter. At the Garden, more than seven thousand distracted fans showed up. Bailey Howell of the Detroit Pistons was the star of the game, scoring twenty-five points, but the Knicks won it by outscoring the Pistons in the fourth period with the help of Donnie Butcher and Dave Budd, two bench players I had never even heard of before that night.

I don't recall much about the game except a feeling that the whole event was surreal. Jumping Johnny Green of the Knicks flew magically into the air for rebounds while gravity held the seven thousand of us in our seats, and our young president had just been shot. Newspapers strewn about the stadium announced, "Kennedy Killed by Sniper." News of the assassination had been played over and over again so many times during that twenty-four hours that the murder seemed to be little more than a nightmare created by the media.

On the subway ride home, I stood holding on to a hand strap and looked over the shoulder of a man reading the front page of the *New York Times*, a story by James Reston: "America wept tonight, not alone for its dead young President, but for itself. The grief was general, for somehow the worst in the nation had prevailed over the best. The indictment extended beyond the assassin, for something in the nation itself, some strain of madness and violence, had destroyed the highest symbol of law and order."

It felt to me then as if the world were coming apart, and perhaps Kennedy's murder *was* the fracture point, for chaos seemed to define the rest of the decade—the murders of Robert Kennedy, Martin Luther King, Jr., and Malcolm X; the slaughter at Kent State; the brutal beatings at the Democratic National Convention in Chicago; the debacle of Vietnam. That year, in 1963, my own home seemed to be exploding into fragments. My father's drinking and his anger matched the times. In our small apartment my mother was the unchanging center.

As my mother and I rode home on the subway that night, I thought about the game, which had been disappointing even though the New York team had won. Richie Guerin no longer played for the Knicks; he had been traded early in the season and now played for the St. Louis Hawks, starring alongside Cliff Hagan and Bob Pettit. After playing only one season in the pros, Tom Stith was also gone from the game: he had averaged only three points per game and shot a dismal 30 percent from the foul line. I was forced to accept the fact that his signs of the cross may have been less an act of faith than one of desperation.

But my mind drifted from the game and, for a reason I couldn't understand, I recalled something that happened to me years before, when I was in the fifth or sixth grade. My mother was in line with other women in Drewsen's Delicatessen, and I was in Lou and Arty's Candy Store paging through the comic books. I came across a new *Superman* that I wanted desperately and ran next door to ask my mother for a dime. In my rush and enthusiasm I didn't notice that the clean plate-glass door to Drewsen's was closed, and I ran through it, spraying glass in front of me. I got up from the floor, unscratched, and looked into the wide eyes of the women in line who gaped at me, stunned and speechless, as if I had just revealed my secret powers. It was my mother who reached down, brushing the shards of glass from my hair and clothes, and asked me if I were all right—able to see, after all, that I was only a boy, her son, who had exploded through a glass door with the passion and unearned luck of youth.

As the train rocked through the tunnel like a time machine that headed back to the Bronx and forward to a dark future, I saw my mother's innocent eyes as she looked back at me with love. It seemed then that no matter what the disaster, she would be able to look back, to face any sadness, to move into the future without forgetting the past. In my mother's eyes—as in Molly's, Loretta's, and many other Bronx women's—was no restless desire for another geography, but a faith in the new world in which she lived from day to ordinary day. As the subway ground slowly to a stop at Bedford Park Station, the window reflected her face and the stained sign that told us we were home.

·····

By the summer of 1986, Letty had been dead for more than a decade. Loretta, suffering from emphysema and having to use a walker, lived by herself in the same apartment overlooking the now untended gardens of the Susan Devin. Most of Loretta's old friends and neighbors were gone. My mother had moved to Vermont.

Loretta was determined to stay in her apartment in the Bronx. Often, her labored breathing rattled through her gaunt frame and shook her memory of the past—the peaceful gardens, the familiar faces, the pleasant exchanges. By the mid-1980s, she was forced to submit to the careless hands and unfocused eyes of Annette Washington, a twenty-eight-year-old home care attendant. Washington, the mother of a nine-year-old boy, did shopping and other chores for Loretta, who, aware of the changes around her in the Bronx, had devised a code of door knocks to avoid robbery.

After work some time during the first week in August, Annette Washington went to Loretta's house and knocked so that Loretta would open her door. Then she entered with her boyfriend, who cut Loretta's throat with two kitchen knives. They ransacked the apartment but found only a small amount of cash and valuables to feed his crack habit. On August 8, Loretta's body was found lying in the foyer not far from the sunken living room.

When I look past the barbed wire that now tops the iron fence in front of the Susan Devin garden and stare at Loretta's window, my only thought is whether she knew, even for a split second, that the world had changed so fast, become so evil. Or did Annette Washington's boyfriend catch her from behind, stop her breathing before she knew it was anything but the emphysema? My nightmares show her turning toward him, twisting her neck around to see the gleaming smile of his blade, her eyes filled with recognition—not fear, but knowledge. In the daylight, as I stand in front of her apartment building, I hope that she never turned, never knew, even though I would have to know, even though I would have to look back. But her story may be a narrative of the most brutal recognition. It may be the story of Lot's wife, a turning back so necessary and painful that it takes our breath away, the future reaching its gnarled hand to tap us on the shoulder.

················

CHAPTER 2

Fathers *and* Sons

Soughing from the north-west on the winedark sea,
and as he felt the wind, Telemakhos called to all
hands to break out mast and sail.
　　　　　　—Homer, *The Odyssey*
　　　　　　　(translated by Robert Fitzgerald)

He felt that although his father loved their home and
loved all of them, he was more lonely than the
contentment of this family love could help.
　　　　　　—James Agee, *A Death in the Family*

This is the third history. It is the history that each
man makes alone out of what is left to him. Bits of
wreckage. Some bones. The words of the dead.
　　　　　　—Cormac McCarthy, *The Crossing*

My father would play the saxophone at dusk in alleyways throughout the Bronx. When the light shimmered between blue and grey, he would seem to slip between the particles and be there in the coal-dusted space among apartment buildings, like a sound in an absolute silence. He was gaunt and unshaven, and the music he made was a moan, such an aching sadness in the notes that the people who came to their back windows smiled. It was the kind of sorrow that made others happy.

If the music made them shiver as they leaned against their window sills, silver rained down like hailstones, and dollar bills floated like paper snowflakes into his upturned cap. He never smiled up at them but continued to play—slowly, softly, letting the melody rise up with the heat.

With the money he collected he took me on adventures around the city. Once we went to Yankee Stadium to watch the Cleveland Indians play New York. It was a contest between Rocky Colavito and Mickey Mantle. Dark against light. East versus West. The ethnic wise guy taking on blond-haired, homogenized America. I probably sided with Mantle. Then, my hair was blond, too. Now I'd root for Colavito. My hair has gotten darker, as has my vision of the world.

The Yankees won that day. Mantle hit a double and a home run. He also hit a pop fly to the infield that was so high it came within an inch or two of defying gravity. It hung in the clouds so long that players began to look at one another and fans began to speculate about miracles. The religious silently prayed, and the superstitious looked over their shoulders. When the ball did finally return to the earth, it shot out of the sunlight and clouds as if it had been thrown back by someone who didn't want to hold up the game any longer.

I was supposed to be a Yankee fan, but even then I think I realized that Colavito was more like me than Mantle was. The Rock was from the Bronx. Mantle was from Commerce, Oklahoma. Colavito had wide, wondering dark eyes. He looked like somebody who had been raised on spaghetti and alleyways. Mantle looked like wheat fields and milk. I loved to watch Colavito place the bat behind his back, rest it on his shoulder blades, and stretch like a kid from Arthur Avenue loosening up before a stickball game.

After the last out, my father asked me whose autograph I wanted—Mantle's or Colavito's. When I told him, he looked over at Rocky, who was making his way to the dugout, and waved. Colavito stopped as if he knew him and waited for us to get down to the first row. My father leaned over the fence and whispered something into his ear, and Colavito turned up to me, signed my outstretched program, and said, "You got it, kid." I wasn't sure what he meant, of course—the autograph or some intangible quality that would make *me* a Rocky Colavito some day—but my father seemed to know.

Another time, my father took me horseback riding out by City Island, a boot-shaped piece of land a mile and a half long and a half-mile wide, off the south shore of Pelham Park in the far eastern part of the Bronx. From the southernmost point of the island, just twelve miles from Manhattan, you could see the skyscrapers rise up toward the clouds. It was like a New England fishing village, with church steeples, narrow cobblestone streets, Victorian homes and clapboard cottages, even though it was only twenty minutes from the apartment complexes near Fordham Road. My father was an electrician on construction jobs around the city, so I was surprised to see how gracefully he rode a horse. The horse I sat upon kept flicking its head back and nipping at my legs. I'd jerk the reins one way, and it would go the other. I watched my father's body move rhythmically with the horse. Mine bounced clumsily against it, pathetically out of synch.

The trails led through the park but eventually came to a road crossing about a mile from the City Island drawbridge. The cars were supposed to stop for the horses, but I didn't have much faith in New York City traffic. I was hesitant in urging my horse forward across the intersection. It reared and left me sitting in the path of an oncoming car. My father, like some slim Western hero, galloped by, casually reached down, lifted me under my arm, and gently placed me in front of him in the saddle.

"You're all right, partner," he said as we headed back to the riding center. His words, even his voice, sounded a bit like Rocky Colavito's.

The next day, my eighth birthday, he told me to get dressed, took me by the hand, and led me down the Grand Concourse.

"Where are we going?" I asked.

"A surprise," he said.

We walked past Poe Park just as the hands of the huge clock on the Dollar Savings Bank tower skipped to 10:30, as if time had held its breath until that very instant when I looked up. At Fordham Road we turned left and went into the RKO-Fordham Theater. The theater was empty except for a dozen of my friends whom my father had gathered together to celebrate with us by watching *The Vikings* with Kirk Douglas and Tony Curtis. It was the right choice for eight-year-old kids: Douglas had his eye gouged out by a hawk, Curtis had his hand severed by a foppish English lord, and a Viking chief, played by Ernest Borgnine, leapt into a den of snarling wolves. And, of course, there was Janet Leigh, a mere two years before her destiny in the shower with Anthony Perkins, with breasts that pointed ferociously at the actors and, as I recall, at me.

We watched the movie three times, drunk on popcorn, candy, sodas, and the rippling light that streamed through the darkness. By the third viewing we tossed popcorn at one another as my father sat in the back row, waving a straw and smiling like Oberon at the chaotic transformation that he had created.

These adventures with my father never really happened. I just wish they had. That doesn't mean that there isn't some truth in them, just not a lot of fact. My father did take me to Yankee Stadium once, but he gave no secret signal to Rocky Colavito. He did take me horseback riding, but I was a toddler, and it was in a corral, and he stood outside and watched. I don't know if he was ever on a horse himself. In 1958 he did take me to the movies—the one and only time he did—but he didn't organize a gathering of my friends. He did on rare occasions play the four-string guitar and the banjo, not the saxophone, and certainly never in alleyways. However, I do recall that saxophone player (there was one) as if I saw him yesterday. He may have been someone's father. For all I know, my father dreamed of making that kind of music in back alleys.

I'm not sure if all fathers are mysteries to their sons, but my father was a mystery to me, a mystery in some ways connected to the Bronx itself, with its rusty-smelling air from bus exhaust and the ever-present shadows off tall buildings. In trying to understand him, I find myself imagining his life before me and with me. Some of us wonder where we should look for our fathers—in what ledgers, in what family albums, in which yearbooks and medals, in what memories? Should we look for them in what happened or in what didn't happen, in the moments that we witnessed or in those hidden from us? In surmise or history?

Before my father died, I thought I understood him very well. He drank because he hated his jobs on construction crews in Queens and Brooklyn and Manhattan. He had had higher aspirations, and the failure of his dreams had worn down his spirit. The jobs, I figured, sent him to Durella's Bar near Villa Avenue. The liquor, I reasoned, brought him home swollen-tongued with rage. Fate made my mother and sister and me the target of his anger. At the time, I assumed it was just all part of what it meant to grow up in the Bronx, a place where women were somehow able to seem content but where men gnawed at their own flesh like wolves caught in steel traps.

As I look back at my father's life, though, I realize that there is more to remember than failures and drink. I recall quite vividly the time he took me fishing on Long Lake in Naples, Maine. Each summer our family would rent the same cabin on the pine-shaded shores along the lake. This particular time was our second summer there, and I was five years old. I don't remember checking the poles, digging for bait, or gathering tackle boxes, but I can see my father, Bill Farmer—the handyman—and myself taking off from the shore in the cool pitch darkness.

The boat, an old wooden inboard, hummed and sputtered when it took off, then settled into a purring as it cut through the black water. Because the trip happened nearly forty years ago in the middle of the night when I was still a bit drunk with sleep, it is like a dream to me now. We headed toward an island about two miles northwest of our dock. In the darkness it appeared to be farther away, unreachable as objects can seem in dreams. The spray from the water felt no more real than a distant memory, an asperges before a high mass. But there was nothing religious about this night: my father never went to church, and Bill Farmer had an ironic twist to his grin, suggesting that he was a man who had long ago given up believing in any meaning he couldn't make up himself. As if to prove his point, he fell off the roof of the main house the next winter and died.

This night, however, was laced with laughter and worms. When we got about two hundred yards off the center of the island, Bill cut the engine and tossed the anchor overboard. For the next four hours we pulled in hundreds of whiskered catfish. They flew, scaleless and wolfish, into the stern. I caught a few, but it was my father who lifted them out of the water, two and three at a time, just by beckoning them with his hand, it seemed. The air filled with the rank perfume of fish and nightcrawlers, a musky scent of earth and death.

An hour before sunrise we had so many fish that the boat was sunken to the water line. When we returned to the dock, people from the town were lined up to gaze at our catch. My father tossed fish to the cheering crowd.

.....

Of course, this story is only half true. Bill Farmer did, as I recall, have an ironic sense of humor. He did fall off a roof the next winter and die. We did catch a lot of catfish—seventy, if you can believe a fisherman's count. But there were no crowds at the dock when we returned. It was still dark. My father did not magnanimously toss fish to the admiring multitudes, and most likely he did not beckon to the catfish, which then leapt suicidally into our boat.

But he did take me fishing, and I remember that, along with his later drinking and sadness. As a child, I felt certain that most of my friends lived the way I did, waiting on week nights for a father's late arrival, knowing what it meant. Many of my friends' fathers labored with their hands from early in the morning until four or five in the afternoon and then went to O'Shea's or the Jolly Tinker for a few on the way home. Some, perhaps, came home at six or seven softly anesthetized. Most, I would guess, stumbled into the living room, as my father often did, and exorcized their demons in front of wife and children, usually confusing these innocents with their own nightmares or sense of failure. On weekends we would wait for the transformation that coincided with the setting of the sun— an eclipse that darkened the personality in a steady, inevitable manner, leading to slurred insults, baleful looks, and an unsteady exit to the bedroom. Those exits were exhilarating for those of us who silently wished for them throughout the evening. In those exits the world was given back to us.

When I was a young child, my father was in his late thirties, slim and handsome, his arms cabled with muscles from working physically every day. At parties he sang in a gentle tenor. He had a wry sense of humor and his cleverness seemed to make all of the adults laugh. Then one day when I was a bit older, I noticed that he didn't laugh much at all, that he sang less, and that he no longer looked slim, but emaciated, like a hollow-eyed survivor of a prison camp.

He didn't change overnight. Perhaps I just didn't notice his sadness, the way it ate the flesh from his bones, until I was stunned by his anger. The first time I noticed it I was about seven years old. My mother had gone into the hospital for a few days to receive treatment for kidney stones. My sister, who was ten, and I were sitting with him at the kitchen table for dinner. I remember three things from that meal. We were eating franks and beans; my father flicked his hand out and slapped my sister in the face; then he looked at me and said, "What kind of a son are you?" Of course, even then I knew it was a statement, not a question. I don't remember why he slapped my sister, but I remember the blood trickling down her face from her nose onto her chin. I remember feeling my mother's absence. Surely, he did too. But I also recall feeling then that words and silences can be as stinging as a slap. My father never apologized. Through the years he never apologized at all for drunkenness or for taking the joy and life out of a room with angry stares or accusatory silences. He could be pleasant and kind at times—maybe performing his own form of penance—but he never apologized.

My mother, sister, and I survived in our own ways. My mother through her love for us. Her eyes stayed on us. My sister escaped through her friends and music. She danced to American Bandstand and talked endlessly with her girlfriends. She leapt into the world, away from my father, away from anger and silence. I discovered words and stories. I found comic books in George and Sarah's Candy Store on 198th Street. I'd be sent there to get my father a package of Chesterfield regulars, and I'd end up by the racks of comics in the back of the store, dreaming about what the ten cents in my pocket would buy me. Like everyone else at the time, I read *Superman* avidly, but I also read *Aquaman* and *Captain Marvel*. Then *Spider-Man, Green Lantern, Captain America, Flash*. Eventually, I followed the battles of Sgt. Rock of Easy Company and the bullwhip-wielding Rawhide Kid.

When I returned home from Sarah's, I barely paused to give my father his unfiltered cigarettes, the cool cellophane sliding out of my hand like ice, before I angled myself into the corner of the couch to read about Clark Kent, Peter Parker, or Billy Batson—all, like me, leading double lives, our real selves hidden from view. After all, I reasoned, Peter Parker was just an ordinary high school student who had been bitten by a radioactive spider, and Billy Batson was simply an orphan who had that one magic word, *Shazam*, to transform him. Without knowing it at the time, I'm certain that I had faith in the magic of words and stories to transform me. Deep down I was convinced that stories could be made to change the world, that if I found the right words, the right stories, I could become strong enough to hold my world in place. I dreamt that I would discover my own story, which would change both me and the world I lived in.

As I got a little older, I read *Archie* and then the *Classics Illustrated*—where I first encountered Stevenson, Defoe, Swift, and Homer. In those comic books, too, I found the legends of William Tell, the Knights of the Round Table, Kit Carson. As I read, the apartment would dissolve. My father would disappear unless his anger rose to such a pitch that my own world fractured, and I found myself once again in the living room, the radiator hissing, the tension swelling, and the interminable waiting until I could return to a truer story than the one my father created for me.

As I got older, I often wondered about my father's story, a story enigmatic to me but one that seemed to control so much of the plot of my own life in the Bronx. I had heard that he had been accepted into MIT, that he had wanted to be an engineer, but that he had needed to help support his family, that he had needed to care for his father. My grandfather had been a few months shy of seventy and blind when my father was born, which may have made him care more deeply for my father, a face that he could know only through his fingertips. And maybe my father loved his own more profoundly, for my grandfather was both father and son from the very beginning, someone to care for and protect as much as look up to. Throughout his teenage years, my father would spend a part of each evening walking with this man, holding his arm as they strolled up and down Grove Street in Brooklyn. I imagine they knew most of the people they passed on those streets. Everyone knew Otto, the tailor, the son of the professor in Russia, whose brothers had served in the Prussian army and won the German Iron Cross. Everyone knew Otto, who, even in his blindness, continued to make fine clothes for the wealthy in Manhattan.

So it was the loss of MIT, I concluded, that ate away at my father through the years. When I got old enough to read Faulkner, I saw my father as kin to the Compsons, destroyed by honor, caring for his family and losing his chance at a career in the process. But then, the image of Quentin Compson nudging my imagination, I wondered what other romantic possibilities there were. Had there been some unrequited love? An older woman who refused to leave her husband? Was there some secret sin, or was he simply unconjugatable, a man who carried an inexplicable sorrow throughout his life? As a child, I think I deeply wanted his sadness not to be a simple one. I wanted his suffering to come from some exotic source, some complex tragedy that would leave me the man I wanted him to be—brave, decent, loving, but unfairly treated by a dark, complicated fate.

I tried to find him in the stories that were given to me. My aunt Mildred said he had been very different before World War II. He had been "carefree and fun loving." His oldest brother, Frank, said he came back from the war another person. This story made sense to me. When I was older, I saw many of my own friends return from Vietnam unrecognizable. They had gone off as garrulous boys and returned as silent men. My father rarely spoke of the war, as if there were no words to explain.

And there was his trip to Montauk. The day after he came back from the South Seas, he left a message on the kitchen table that he needed some time by himself. He resurrected an old bike from the shadows and cobwebs of the basement of his parents' brownstone, let the wooden door close without looking back at his distorted reflection in the beveled glass, and took off from 1714 Grove Street in Brooklyn, heading northeast past the storefronts and scattered developments of Queens and into the narrowing claw of land that led to the North and South Shores of Long Island.

He rode more than one hundred miles on the fat old tires that were already a bit bleached with wear and cracked by dry rot. Although much of his journey was over flat land, many times in the days to come he must have wished for several speeds so that he could have shifted gears and eased his way up the gentle inclines. He must have wondered if he were heading toward his future or outdistancing his past as he floated through towns whose names were magically different from the ones in Brooklyn—Patchogue, Quogue, Center Moriches—and into a world reminiscent of *The Great Gatsby* in East Hampton, Amagansett, and Montauk.

His old surname, Persanowski, which he had shed when he was barely eighteen, seemed no part of this landscape, with its ocean breezes and desolate dunes. The name he and his brothers had discarded because it sounded Jewish, a drawback in the business world even when you were really Lutheran, named nothing in this place, least of all him as he glided along as thoughtless and wordless as a gull.

When he reached the farthest point of land, night was beginning to fall, and he looked to the left toward New England and to the right into the blank Atlantic. Then he let go of his bicycle, shed his clothes, and stepped naked into the iridescent sea. He loved the salt water, and when he dove in, the world disappeared, replaced by a cold, dark-green nothingness. The water clung to him like moonlight, and when he rose and shook his head, sparks flew into the darkness. He stood there looking back at the empty land, per-haps recognizing for a moment the stubborn truths that make doubts and fears seem insignificant.

Most of this story is true. My father did disappear for two weeks after the war, taking off on a bike to Montauk. He and his three brothers had changed their name in the early 1930s. As were many men who came back from Europe or the South Pacific after World War II, he was changed, I suspect, even more profoundly than when he had discarded his name at the courthouse. My father, like many of the men of his generation, might have found it difficult to find a relationship between the two decades—the 1940s and the 1950s—one defined by depression and death, the other by a dizzy-ing optimism and sense of possibility.

Like many others, he staggered into this new life, trying to match the advertising slogans for the future with the world he had just left behind. Most of my friends' fathers, it seemed to me as a young boy, were taciturn, sad-eyed men. Never did they laugh up-roariously or play stickball with us on the sidewalks. Rarely did they stroll the neighborhood. They worked, they spent time in the bars, they read the newspapers. They refused to be anything but stolid, inexplicable, and always, in some way, absent.

The only father we knew who was not gruff or distant was my friend Jimmy's. He always had a smile or a kind word. It was all the more shocking, then, when we were in high school and discovered one Friday afternoon that he had been found unconscious from an overdose of pills on Central Avenue in Yonkers. A note pinned to his shirt stated that he was sorry, but he couldn't stand his wife anymore. We all wondered then, I suppose, what nightmares these other, more silent men suppressed.

The only other men we knew were the brothers and the priests. The brothers seemed more human, more accessible. The priests we saw only at mass or confirmation or special celebrations in school.

They were kindly, avuncular, but somehow not real men, closer to apparitions. The brothers taught us. Brother Gwyn and Brother Bruce teased us about girlfriends, laughed at our jokes, talked about sports. And even if a few, like Brother Boniface, took sadistic pleasure in the pain they were able to create, the rest seemed good men—strict, but much like older male siblings. Never fathers, though, because, like priests, they were separate from the rest of the world, chosen to be different, another mystery of maleness that nobody could explain to us.

The brothers often showed us a humor and a kindness that our fathers did not, a gentleness and strength that led us into the world, but it was our fathers whom we needed to understand. We had trouble finding *their* meaning in what they said because they said so little, and when they drank, the anger seemed so incommensurate, exploding from a source larger than our experience allowed us to imagine.

My father was often silent. He would stare sullenly from his living room chair, or he would read the newspaper at the kitchen window and look up occasionally to watch people pass by in front of the apartment building. Silence can often speak more clearly than words, and he was invariably silent after he fought with a foreman and quit a job. But silence typically led to drink and drink to more words, enough to slowly fill a small room, breath by breath squeezing the air into a corner.

These are also my father's stories:

Home at noon. This meant he had fought with someone on a job and had "packed his tools." Silence followed.

Silence turned to apprehension, a fear of going back to work, a new job, another set of bosses, another group of bricklayers, plumbers, laborers.

.....

Fear turned to drink. Drink to anger. Then sleep. A sleep beyond nightmares. A sleep that numbed all the pain. With unemployment came a sort of narcolepsy until he was drawn by necessity back to the world. However, as the years went along, the periods between job losses became shorter, and the periods of sleep became longer. Then, one day, a year or two before I left the house, there were no more jobs. Unemployment just drifted into early retirement.

Twenty-five years remained for him at the kitchen table with the newspaper. Looking up from current events during those years, he must have pondered his own past.

He graduated from Newtown High School in Brooklyn, an honor student with an A average, a member of the Arista Society. In his yearbook they summed him up as "an all 'round good fellow," as if the editors had to rely on the vaguest generalizations because they did not really know him. His destination was listed as "college," but he was soon to be accepted into MIT.

Family responsibilities and work intruded on his plans. He joined the International Brotherhood of Electrical Workers. Maybe he hoped that they, too, would prove to be a group of all around good fellows. Then the war started. In March 1943 he was part of the Seventy-fourth Naval Construction Battalion that formed at Camp Peary in Williamsburg. Along with his fellow recruits, he wended his way from Camp Davis in Endicott, Rhode Island, to Camp Parks in California, then on to Pearl Harbor and the islands of the South Pacific. He was part of the campaigns on Okinawa and Tarawa and the Marshall Islands. In October 1945 he brought home a bronze star and his Seabees yearbook.

In an elliptical way, that book tells his story. Besides photographs of each company and platoon in his battalion, the album is filled with pictures from the campaigns. There are images of sun-scorched islands, the white-hot sun leaving nothing unexposed—the bomb craters, the rusting metal, the few shattered palm trees, the sun-blistered corpses. There seem to be no shadows, only an inescapable, blinding white heat. Amidst the views of crumbling cinder block and debris from the invasions are photographs of the enemy dead. The disembodied head of a Japanese officer—charred black, the mouth flung wide, frozen in a scream, the teeth hanging precariously in rotted gums—stares blindly from one of the pages. In another, a Japanese soldier, caught in the act of climbing from an underground tunnel, his forearms propped against the ledge of the opening, has been melted by a flame thrower into a dark fury that not even the tropical sun can lighten.

But in all the photographs of my father, he is smiling. He is slim and tan. Blond streaks course through his hair like rivulets of sunlight. Most of the men are smiling, it seems, and I wonder if my father had been unnerved by the horror of war or shattered by the promise of it when he returned a few years later. Was it, finally, for him the worst of times or the best? Those photographs picture a men's club, bottles of beer, cartons of cigarettes, a shirtless camaraderie in which nearly everyone is equal and joined together for a grand purpose with a boyish sense of irony strong enough even to shade them from the sun.

What could match this collection of all around good fellows? Where again could they find this union of English Romanticism and 1940s science? When my father returned to the United States, he came home to another life, to a new wife, then to children—to simple work. Perhaps living through the war had been easy compared with living an ordinary Thursday afternoon.

A few years after he got back, he was nearly electrocuted when someone accidentally threw a power switch while he held live wires. He felt as if he had been struck by lightning or burnt by a

flame thrower until a coworker tackled him away from the powerful embrace of those currents. In another accident the ring finger on
his right hand was crushed, then needed to be amputated when
gangrene set in. Just as that electricity seemed to rise up in him
in moments of anger, that missing finger seemed to remind him
of some deeper loss, but I'm not certain he ever knew what that
was.

Somewhere between the lines of these stories is my father's life.
The point where his past and future intersected, where anticipation
and frustration canceled each other out. In his eyes I saw dreams
unrealized, lost through time.

Once, though, I believe, he had a desperate exuberance, a belief
in himself and the world. Once he may have assumed, like Gatsby,
that he could fashion himself from his own Platonic conception.
Once he believed that his own strength and speed and courage
could shape his experience.

One day when my father was seventeen, he sat with his father in
the kitchen of their home. My grandfather cocked his head in my
father's direction as if he heard him say something. His blank eyes
looked through my father's. Then my grandfather stood up as if he
were about to make a speech. But no words came. The wisdom he
then had to offer was not in words. The lesson he taught was the
final one that each father teaches his son. As he stood up, he
clutched his chest and looked futilely ahead. Then, without a
sound, he fell to the ground. My father ran for the doctor, blocks
away, his heart beating fast in fear and love. For those few minutes
he was blind like his father, thinking only of him, hearing only the
explosions in his father's heart. He ran to save him, the three-story
brownstones rushing past him in a blur of colors. Probably, he ran
toward Myrtle Avenue, past a stream of shoppers and into the

bright lights and lines of stores just beyond Bleecker and Menahan Streets. When he returned with the doctor, his father was dead.

Right before my father was taken into the Seabees, he failed the physical for the army. They said he had a heart murmur. For the next half century he talked about his "bum ticker," and although I believe he knew his heart was strong, he felt some part of it had burst with his own father's. In some way he envied his father's blindness, a special sort of seeing he was never able to reinvent for himself. Kierkegaard once said that if a man cannot forget, he will never amount to much. Whatever my father amounted to, there was something he was never able to forget.

On March 3, 1994, my father died, like his father, of a stroke to the heart, a flash of blinding light in which for a moment, perhaps, he saw that he had been right all along: his heart was not strong enough. Who knows if anybody's heart is ready for what the world will offer?

As I write these words, I imagine my father running through the streets of Brooklyn in an impossible attempt to save his father— running until years later he found himself not very far away in the Bronx, not sure what had been salvaged in a place that, perhaps, induced even more dreams of running. But maybe in that first desperate run when he was seventeen, he saved some piece of himself instead, a true story: a piece of his fragile heart, evidence that he was more mysterious and stubbornly human than any story, fact or fiction, can ever tell.

·····

My father left the Bronx in the summer of 1978. He left in the early morning before the heat turned soggy and everything looked limp with moisture and regret. The featureless moving van took the furniture, and my father stepped out of the apartment he had lived in for thirty years and never even thought of looking back. He never returned. He left for Burlington, Vermont, to an apartment with a view of Camel's Hump jutting above the rest of the Green Mountains.

If he would have turned back on that early summer's morning, he might have seen the half-open slats of the venetian blinds in the kitchen window, his observation post on the world. Perhaps he would have noticed the dirty brick darkening into a blurred gray. He might have wondered what the view from his new apartment could offer him, how what he would see could possibly change the man he had become. He surely knew that he would never see the landscape of the Bronx again, the buses puffing up the Grand Concourse, the window glass shivering as the subway roared beneath him, the teenagers leaning adroitly against car doors, the stooped women dragging their shopping carts like sleds along the iceless streets.

In his new apartment was a new window, looking out onto a quieter street than he was used to, with only an occasional bus or car or pedestrian. Each morning he sat at that window, an unfiltered cigarette poised between his index and middle fingers, the smoke curling around them and over the stump of his ring finger. Usually, there was a half-filled can of beer near his ash tray and the newspaper. His coiled muscles had turned skeletal, purple bruises always tattooed his thin arms, but his sandy hair had turned a darker brown, not grey, and his eyes had more irony than anger in them. Occasionally, a playful sense of humor sprang from him, as if he were remembering what he was like as a boy, a young man who knew that there was no difference between blindness and sight. Now, what he saw was not the Bronx he had left in 1978, but the one from the early 1950s, a Bronx that promised escape to Maine, perhaps. By 1978 he had no hope of leaving the Bronx behind, so he took it with him. Out the window he saw it. He saw himself hitting fungoes to Patty Dougherty and me at Harris Field on a Saturday afternoon in August. He saw himself leading me by the hand past the printing presses at the *Herald Tribune,* pointing out the electrical work he had done, introducing me to the old timers who tousled my blond hair with their ink-stained hands. He saw himself as he once was in the Bronx, dreaming of his summers in Maine, hiking along the shortcut—a path through the pine woods to town, a shaggy-haired dog named Tippy and me trailing behind him. In those strolls he believed, as I had, that anything was possible, that an afternoon's walk could take forever, that love might be available without even asking for it, that there was more future than there would ever be past.

As he looked out his new window, he saw how much of the past was his future, and he gazed at it each day, not so much understanding it, but just remembering—as if the past, the Bronx itself, were indecipherable, a territory that could never be truly charted. For me, the Bronx had always seemed a precisely known world, both safe and claustrophobic. No map was necessary. My father, though, was dark and mysterious, demanding to be understood, but resisting understanding in every contour. At some point in time it seemed that he could be only what we imagined him to be. It was like having a map but not the landscape that was its reference.

The last time I saw my father was a few months before he died. He sat at his kitchen table, looking out the window. The look in his eyes was faraway, his mouth turned up in the promise of a smile. His expression reminded me of a few minutes we spent together in the Bronx decades before. He had stood on the roof of our apartment building, dusk had washed away the blazing summer sun, and a purple coolness was descending around us. The tar, which a few hours before had appeared to sizzle, was still warm and as soft as putty. He knelt before the bent trunk of the television antenna, whispering curses, the muscles in his forearms and biceps knotting together as he righted it and replaced the screws in the base. The upper part of the antenna hung over him like a strange parody of an oak sapling, metallic and dangerous. He straightened it, reattached the wires, and stepped back for a moment to observe his work. We stood there together, a few feet from the dizzying edge of the roof, people and cars speckling the roads and sidewalks below us, the Bronx stretching out north and south and west in front of us. He touched my shoulder, his fingers alighting on it as weightless as a moth, and mused aloud, "I wonder what the poor people are doing today?" He smiled as he looked out at the other rooftops, at the Bronx, as if he had climbed a mountain peak and had earned some droll remark. As a young child, I wondered if we were rich and if the Bronx might not be as close to paradise as anyone could expect to come.

....

PART TWO

Dreaming *of* Columbus

In his cosmographical ideas Columbus remained
stubbornly and obstinately, to the end of his life,
absolutely and completely wrong.

—Samuel Eliot Morison,
Admiral of the Ocean Sea

It's not down in any map; true places never are.

—Herman Melville, *Moby Dick*

CHAPTER 3

···············

Boys

Lads that thought there was no more behind
But such a day tomorrow as today
And to be boy eternal.
       —William Shakespeare, *The Winter's Tale*

There are two things that you can learn only by rote:
grammar and religion.
       —Jimmy Breslin, *Once a Catholic*

and what I want to know is
how do you like your blueeyed boy
       —e. e. cummings, "Buffalo Bill's"

Rudy Figuera never lost a spelling bee in his eight years at St. Philip Neri Elementary School. Except for that achievement, he would have been consistently, overpoweringly unexceptional. Granted, he looked a bit like a frog, bug-eyed and flat-mouthed, but not so amphibian as to cause snickers or attract much notice. His voice was hoarse, and he croaked out those letters, S E P A R A T E, like a bullfrog at the edge of a pond and remained standing as all of the others fell from the circle back into their seats. Rudy never said much unless he was in a spelling contest. Now that I think back on it, I don't recall his ever saying *anything* in those eight years. His voice, with a rasping sadness to it, uttered letters, never whole words or complete sentences. He would stand in the playground watching everything from a wistful distance, and in the classroom he would smile pointlessly throughout the day. In general, he wasn't a good student. As a matter of fact, he was one of the worst in the class, but no one could outspell him.

Spelling gave Rudy a hold on the world, and as we drifted through the late 1950s and into the early 1960s, we all needed something to offset the fear that the world could be altered, perhaps disappear, at any moment. For many of us at St. Philip's, Rudy's spelling was a fixed point in a changing world. If the bomb drill sounded, and we squeezed under our desks or crouched, arms tight around our knees, in the hallways, we always knew that Rudy would return to the classroom to spell all of his words correctly. As we were slowly transformed into existentialists, Rudy may have been the only one in the class who, without hesitation, could have spelled such a word.

It was on a Tuesday, a spelling bee day, that we first heard about the blockade of Cuba. Of course, we all knew about the missile situation in a vague way; it threatened like a distant thunder. It had been threatening for days, rumbling through the news and in our parents' conversations. Monday night, Kennedy made his speech: "The cost of freedom is always high, but Americans have always paid it. And one path we shall never choose, and that is the path of surrender, or submission." By Tuesday morning we all knew about the blockade. We knew it was serious, deserving of the name *crisis,* not because of the president's speech or editorials in the *Daily News,* which most of us read only for the sports scores, but because so many of our mothers went to church that morning. Everyone in the neighborhood seemed to be clutching rosary beads.

Six of us were left standing in a broken circle around the room that day, but Joe Pagano was about to slide into his seat as soon as he accepted the fact that he had no idea how to spell *embarrassment*: was it two Ms, one R, or one S and two Rs, or two of everything, including Bs? Pagano hitched up his belt, which was already around his chest, and looked soulfully around the room, but those faces offered no solace and certainly no answers. Billy Brown, who was next in line, wore a smug grin that told us he knew how to spell the word, but I'm fairly certain most us of hoped he would fail, for we despised his annoying propriety—he always did his homework, he always raised his hand, he even took notes in Brother Placid's class while the rest of us dreamed or talked or played elaborate tricks on one another. By our standards, Billy Brown was learned without being interesting, good without being kind, obedient but not brave. Obedience seemed to be the principal virtue we were taught, but most of us sensed that courage came from disobedience.

We all worshiped bravery, perhaps because there were so many things that we were scared of in our lives. We were scared of failing and maybe even of succeeding, of leaving the Bronx one day or of never having the opportunity to get away, of a war occurring, or worse even, no dramatic event coming along to break up the flat plain that the plot of our lives might otherwise resemble. For most of us, life seemed to be a series of anticlimaxes, and perhaps we were afraid not that the world would end, but that it already had and we had not noticed. Brother Bruce came into the room and said "bomb drill" before Joe Pagano had the chance to add the second B that he was almost surely hesitating over, and we marched out of the room wondering if Khrushchev had sent a missile our way, if Rudy Figuera would ever again have the chance to beat Billy Brown, if we would be buried like martyrs under the stones of St. Philip Neri.

We sat in the hallway, backs against the cool cinder block, as we waited for the whisper of metal and the blinding flash that would answer all of our questions. I pictured the blaze of light that would come, a fireball that would print our images on the walls like murals, silhouettes left behind by the radioactive cloud that would mushroom magnificently into the sky. A few months before, I had read John Hersey's *Hiroshima,* and as I sat in the hallway, I tried to remember his representations of that explosion of light—terrible, noiseless, a gigantic photographic flash, whiter than white, a brilliant yellow—but mainly I recalled his description of a young woman who worked in an office building. The light she saw paralyzed her with fear, and she lost consciousness as everything around her fell—mainly bookcases, a shower of books falling through the otherworldly whiteness until she was crushed. I couldn't see her face, though. For some reason, the faces I saw were not family and friends or characters from *Hiroshima,* but Ole Miss students—short haired and red faced, screaming at a fragile-looking black man who was walking toward a building on the campus. At that time I wasn't sure exactly what was going on in the images I had seen on the television screen, but something in those white faces, raw and scarred with hate, frightened me as much as the bomb. It was those faces that I saw frozen in that terrible light.

The bomb did not drop on us that afternoon, but for the rest of that week we waited for it to come. We saw our mothers go to church in the mornings, and we gathered in the hallways to prepare for the end of the world. It haunted us in the classroom and the schoolyard. We realized, I think, that nothing could save us—not Rudy Figuera's unerring spelling, not our mothers' prayers, not our games. Nevertheless, we valued our mothers' faith, prized Rudy's uncanny spelling, and played our games anyway, more passionately, perhaps, because the apocalypse seemed so close at hand. Games were our poems. They had form and shape amid the shapeless stretch of time. They had rules and boundaries. We acted out our fears and dreams as if we were characters in a book.

By the next week, Khrushchev was defeated, out-bluffed, shown to be a shoe-banging bully and not the handsome hero John F. Kennedy was for us. But even with a hero who played touch football on the beaches of Cape Cod and whose smile suggested that the world would yield to our wishes if we were graceful enough, most of us no longer believed in the inevitability of such grace, except perhaps in games. And we played our games with great fury and love. The Bronx of that time seemed bounded by games. Trees served as landmarks in ring-a-levio. Manhole covers marked bases for stickball. Chalk colored the sidewalks. Games gave a structure to our days, a shape, a rhythm to anticipation, an aesthetic for the commonplace.

The day after the bomb didn't drop we played Johnny-on-the-pony in the schoolyard during lunch hour. It had just the right amount of savagery mixed with strategy to suit our postapocalyptic mood. When we chose up sides, we had eight against the other team's seven because we had to pick Tommy Murray, pale skinned and whining and too skinny to do any damage. Being light and agile were advantages in the game, but you needed to be athletic and daring, too. Murray was neither, and he had a habit of looking around skittishly as if he expected to be poked and pushed from every corner. Because he expected it, he was.

The great Johnny-on-the-pony players had to abandon themselves to the air, or they had to dare the weight of the world to fall on their backs. The rules of the game were simple. First, certain players, like Vincent Calabria, who weighed one hundred ninety pounds by the fifth grade, were banned from ordinary games. Then, one team lined up against the fence, one player standing upright and the others bending down in front of him to form a horse. Each boy wrapped his arms tightly around the waist of the boy in front of him, a touching that would have been taboo under any other circumstances. Unlike girls, who sometimes held hands as they walked along the streets or held each other as they danced, the boys I knew would have rather stood naked in church than have touched another boy's hand or waist. But in Johnny-on-the-pony there they were, bent over each other, chins pressed against the sides of buttocks, hands grazing groins. The other team stood back about twenty yards and decided the order of the jumps. Usually, one team decided that the other had a weak point, and they tried to focus on that spot, placing as many bodies on the back of that boy as possible. Once all the boys were on the pony, they chanted, "Johnny on the pony, one, two, three . . . one, two, three." If the horse held the weight, they shook the riders off and had their turn.

This particular game was not an ordinary one because, except for Tommy Murray, only the biggest, along with the most athletic boys in the class, were engaged in the contest. For our team, Tommy Murray was the fence pillow, a position that demanded absolutely no athletic ability, no strength. He was nothing but a cushion; however, if the opposing jumpers leapt across the line of backs, they came toward him, and even if they didn't hit him full on, forearms extended like fenders on a truck, when they landed, the body that took the weight quivered, sending the shock waves forward until it snapped Tommy against the fence. That punishment, of course, was nothing compared to the force of a body landing on your back, sometimes knees first, with a sharp thud that made your legs tremble.

Eugene Euvino jumped first. He weighed nearly as much as Joseph Calabria. The five or ten pounds he lacked to place him in Calabria's legendary weight class for us probably meant little to the boy who had to hold him on his back. Eugene's feet were like webs that grew at oblique angles from his heavy legs, so when he ran, it truly looked as if he were lumbering, as if his flesh were shaking back and forth, making a noise like sheets flapping in the wind. When he fell onto the backs of the first and second boys in line, the air flew from them and their knees buckled and then shook as they locked them straight to hold him up.

Next was Jimmy Bufano, older than the rest of us, tall, lean, and athletic. He always had a suicidal grin on his face, but now it seemed fitting. He backed up ten or fifteen yards behind the point where Eugene had started and flew over him like a gull gliding above a beached whale. He soared over my head, and his right knee and left elbow dug into the boy holding onto Tommy Murray. Billy Slattery grazed my head with the scuffed tip of his black shoes as he landed on the boy in front of me. Johnny "Mizer" DeCaprio landed on the small of my back and pressed down, assisted by gravity and a slight rocking motion. Then one after another they came until two other boys were balanced atop Eugene. As they chanted, "Johnny on the pony, one, two, three," the line of boys holding them began to sway under the weight like cantilevers separating from their supports, and then they toppled into a pile of scraped arms and muffled curses—suffocated, pressed into the asphalt, but exuberantly alive, untouched by anything more serious than an elbow or knee, and able finally to extricate themselves for another game.

In games, we held the world at arm's length and practiced for it as well. We played Hunter, as primitive as any game played with skull and sticks by ancient South American tribes. One person stood against a crowd that charged at him, pushed and knocked until he caught one, and then others were caught, and finally the situation was reversed, one prey and many hunters. We played punchball and stickball, the earth and rubber smell of Spaldeens always on our hands. After school we played football and baseball and basketball. In the summer we played ring-a-levio, and in the winter we attacked each other with snowballs. We tossed them from rooftops on unsuspecting pedestrians. In the fall we took chestnuts from a tree at the end of the Concourse, punched a hole through them, and tied a string around them so that we could smash one against another, the weaker ones exploding into fibers. We played stoopball and tag and hide-and-seek. When the world did not threaten us enough, we leapt across the open chasm between one five-story apartment building and another. We watched the old men play chess in Poe Park or boccie on Villa Avenue and the girls jump rope or pirouette across a hopscotch board. We melted wax and crayons into bottle caps to play skelly and flipped our most prized baseball cards onto the breeze.

We found our games not only in parks and playgrounds, but in alleyways and subway tunnels, in the angles of shadow left under fire escapes, in the recesses of dumbwaiters, in vacant lots and construction sites. The bomb had not dropped, and we searched for ways of living in the world that was left to us. On one sultry May evening, the sort that reminded us that if things were fair, school would be canceled and we would be free for the summer, Patty Dougherty, Steve Tarnok, and I walked aimlessly along Bedford Park Boulevard—silently, each dreaming, like Tom Sawyer, I suppose, about some different adventure. The light from a half moon played woozily on the framework of a new building going up across the street from St. Philip Neri on the Grand Concourse. We all realized at the same time, and without saying a word to one another, what we would do next.

We saw the night watchman sitting near the shed that held the northern corner of the building like a guardhouse. He wore glasses and had gray hair, and a cold stub of cigar was stuck in his mouth. He was squat and perfectly ordinary except for his eyes, which shone with something like a playful knowledge in the gathering darkness. We watched those eyes as we headed toward the side of the building, toward a ditch that we leapt across to get to one of the open windows on the first floor.

By the time we crawled over the grimy sill into the unfinished room, the darkness had fallen with the suddenness of a sharp sound, but actually the only sounds were the hissing of our breath and whispers and the scraping of our sneakers against wood shavings and sheetrock dust on the floor. The building seemed less like a construction site than a site of destruction, the debris suggesting a bombed-out building. As we explored through the unlit corridors, occasionally we glimpsed the figure of the thick night watchman drift past a window, a figure in our game. We climbed the open stairways, picked up stray nails and bits of wood. We covered every room on every floor, as serious as building inspectors.

After an hour or so, the place became too secure, a clubhouse instead of a house of horrors. In the heart of darkness in the center of the building on the second floor, we talked.

"Let's toss some stuff off the roof," Patty said.

"No, let's leave some messages for the workers when they get here tomorrow," I suggested.

But it was Steve who struck the right chord.

"Let's wait until the watchman passes right beneath the window and then jump out behind him."

A ten-foot jump down and outward to the sidewalk and a tree branch to the right of the window made timing crucial. We had to wait for the watchman to pass by, but not far enough by where he would have no chance of catching us if we slipped or stumbled or simply lost our nerve and failed to jump. We also had to choose to see who would go first, the least threatening leap, then second, and finally, and most frightening, third. Patty went first, then Steve, then I was to go.

As we lay there waiting, my heart knocked against my chest, and blood drummed in my ears. It was the sort of moment that seemed to make life worth living. We might break our legs as we leapt into the semidarkness. The night watchman might grab one of us—or two, perhaps—and beat us senseless, tie us in his shack, slit our throats, shoot us with a snub-nosed revolver he hid beneath his shirt. It wasn't likely, but it was possible. And we lived in the world of possibility, perhaps as our fathers once had. It took about ten minutes before he appeared at the north corner again and headed south past the window where we followed his movements. As he walked along, his gaze drifted right and left, but never upward where he would see us. Patty slid into position, raised himself up, and leaned by the left side of the window frame. Steve stood by the right side, and I crouched behind him.

The smell of sawdust and sheet rock mixed with metal filled the night air. Kneeling there, I felt the edge of a moist two-by-four that sparkled in a scrap of moonlight. Without any warning, Patty jumped, seconds after the man passed under the window. Right away I knew that he had jumped too soon, that there would not be enough time for each of us to leap out onto the Concourse before the man could turn and be in position to catch one of us. Patty landed with a thud and an exhalation of breath. Startled, the man turned as Steve flew out of the darkness, beaked like a strange bird. The man stepped toward them, and I was left with no space between him and the two boys. So I did the only thing that was left for me to do: as the watchman stepped past the target of my jump, I flew behind him. He must have sensed my shadow, and certainly he felt the rush of air as I brushed the hairs on the back of his neck. At least, at the time I was sure that I had come that close. My arm snapped a branch, and I landed in a crouch. When he spun around, I dashed past him and joined my friends.

We ran and ran, through alleyways and around parked cars, down Bainbridge Avenue and back onto the Concourse. The man looked old to me, but he chased us without tiring it seemed. He was not fast, but each time we turned, he was there behind us at the same distance. So we ran for minutes, but it could have been hours, days, months, a whole lifetime. We fell in love with this man who chased us, loved him for chasing us, for taking us seriously, for wanting to hunt us down, for entering into our game and connecting it to the adult world. We loved him for his stamina, for making us breathless, for forcing our blood to surge. The streets, old, familiar ones, seemed wonderfully foreign to me as we ran down Valentine and Briggs, past the brothers' house and in the shadow of the church steeple. As I ran, I knew that it was the running I loved and the memory of it, even before it was a memory. And I think we were heartbroken when the old watchman stopped abruptly on 203rd Street and the Grand Concourse. He just stood there for a minute and looked at us as we waited on the corner of the next block. He didn't say anything. He just stared. Our chests heaved as we stared back at him, waiting, expecting him to begin running again, to chase us around the entire Bronx, through the Botanical Gardens, over the fence to the zoo, out past the flatlands of Pelham Parkway, in a looping, infinite circle. Instead, he turned and headed south. We slipped behind a line of parked cars and followed him back toward the construction site.

But he didn't stop when he came to his shack, and he didn't stop at his building. He walked right past and kept on going. We waited as he crossed the Bedford Park Boulevard overpass. When he walked over 200th Street, we ran across the overpass and snuck once again behind a line of cars. He kept on marching down the Concourse. When he got to 199th Street, I began to get a strange feeling in my stomach. My apartment was on the next block, but, of course, that could not be the direction he was heading.

As his foot touched the corner of my street, time slowed down. With each step, I pondered the possibilities. Did he know me? No, I had never seen him before. Was he a long-lost uncle? A seer? A messenger of God? As a Catholic, I knew such messengers were all around, and it stood to reason that my time had come to meet one. But even when my darkest superstitions rose up, I knew, as he came within a few yards of 2902 Grand Concourse in the middle of 198th Street, he would walk right past and head farther down the block and make a turn, perhaps on Valentine Avenue, and open the door to one of the two-family houses in that neighborhood, that a grey-haired woman in a flowered dress and a dull white apron stained with tomato sauce would greet him, and he would disappear from my life forever.

But he didn't head farther south. Instead, he began to angle in the direction of my apartment building. At first I thought my eyes were playing tricks on me, that in the darkness he only appeared to be turning toward the left. The arc he made toward my building was as slow and flickering as a film shown frame by frame. He seemed to move and stop with each inhalation and exhalation I made, and for a moment I wondered if I could stop time and freeze his movements if I held my breath. When he came to the steps of my building, though, I knew that I was doomed. When he walked up the steps, opened the heavy iron-laced front doors, and put his hand on the brass banister, I knew he was going to march straight up to my apartment, ring the bell, and explain sadly to my parents that I was a juvenile delinquent.

I couldn't see behind the curtain of the inner door. From where I stood, behind a parked car in front of my kitchen window, I could see nothing but flutterings of light. There was nothing for me or Steve or Patty to do but run off again, this time to Mosholu Park, to discuss my sad fate. We couldn't figure out how this man knew as much as he did or what was in store for me when I went home, but I could see in their eyes that they were pleased not to be me. I spent the rest of the evening playing basketball at P.S. 8, dunking on the eight-foot basket, leaping into the air as if I had become a man and left the uncertainties of boyhood beneath me.

When I did return home, no one said anything to me about my behavior. No mention was ever made of a mysterious night watchman, and I never saw the man again—at the construction site or near my apartment building. It was as if he disappeared or never existed, as if I had imagined him, but I suggest nothing symbolic or supernatural about him or the situation. I have no idea who he was, whether he spoke with my parents or visited someone else in the building that night. But if I had invented him that night, he could not have given me and my friends more pleasure, more terror and mystery, a more thrilling game to play.

School and church, like our other games, had familiar rules and rituals. We wore our white suits for Holy Communion and our red jackets for confirmation. We chanted in response to the priest's questions and warily accepted the bishop's ritual slap. In unison we sang out answers in geography and history lessons. Church and school were, for us, deeply connected. In church there were palms and Easter lilies, stained glass windows and crucifixes, pools of holy water and confessional boxes. A dark, brooding mystery permeated every stone of the building. A strange otherness breathed the same air that made the candles flicker. On Sundays, priests wore exotic robes and spoke in a magical language—"Dominus Vobiscum . . . Et cum spiritu tuo . . . Kyrie, eleison . . . Christe, eleison . . . In nomine Patris, et Filii, et Spiritus Sancti."

In school the nuns and brothers floated through our lives, scattering the pieces of sunlight that fell into the classroom during the day. In their ancient garments they seemed dark apparitions, avatars, druidical mysteries of faith personified and clothed in secrets and black liquid robes. For them, we read aloud, made numbers on the board, repeated answer for question, diagrammed sentences, and spoke the words that by rote we had been taught to memorize. Much of this learning was worthwhile, teaching us discipline and sacrifice and a care for details, the ability to singlemindedly focus our attention. But much of this activity was also deadly dull and more concerned with obedience and loyalty to an idea than it was with any genuine learning.

In Brother Placid's class in the seventh grade we created a game that became legend within days, a moment that we talked about and laughed over for years to come, a harmless rebellion that suggests, perhaps, the gentle nature of those times and our desire to find a way to escape our boundaries into the more dangerous world. Brother Placid had been our geography teacher for a few weeks, replacing someone who went on leave and then never returned. He was unremarkable in almost every respect. He was short and stocky, the features of his face ran together like a too familiar landscape, and his glasses gave his eyes a distant, unfocused appearance. When I looked at him, I felt as if everything blurred for a moment. He seemed to be submerged in holy water, but most of us could never decide whether he was saint or fool.

His class was inconceivably boring. Even as I think about his class now, it's difficult to recapture the matchless dullness that he always achieved. He could take the most dramatic subject—the Romans conquering the ancient world—and drone on about it until it seemed as tedious as a bus ride around the neighborhood. He also had the ability to make the simplest subject seem complicated beyond comprehension. Shortly after he took over the class, we spent a full two weeks listening to him lecture in a hoarse whisper about the milk industry in New York State. He required that we take meticulous notes about different types of cows and forty-gallon milk cans and trucks and highways until the very thought of milk made most of us dizzy. We depended upon Billy Brown or Frankie Bartoletti to take careful notes so that the rest of us could daydream about the atomic bomb or the New York Giants.

When Brother Placid came into the classroom one afternoon, his eyes squinting behind glasses thicker than the walls of a bomb shelter, all forty-six of us leaned forward a bit to hear his soft voice as he began reviewing the process by which milk found its way from outlying farms to local grocery stores. "Forty-gallon cans . . . loaded onto trucks . . . highways to the city," his voice ticked on, slightly louder than the clock on the wall. When he turned his back on us and began to write notes on the board, the movement started.

As far as I could tell, no one person moved first. Rather, everyone seemed to move at the same time, as if some group instinct were at work. Forty-six desks squeaked forward. Brother Placid continued to unfurl a ribbon of words from his mouth onto the board. The desks continued to move. When he turned around to face the class, minutes later, his eyes narrowed further into a slit of confusion. All forty-six desks were squeezed up to the front of the room, within a few inches of him, barely room for a slight breeze between his robes and the first line of students.

He never said anything. I looked at his enigmatic face but could not tell if we had tripped him into catatonia or if his saintly instincts allowed him to rise above such worldly absurdity. At any rate, he never said anything. He turned back to the board and started writing notes again. The next time he turned around he nearly fell forward into the gaping space in front of him. All of the desks were crammed into the rear of the room, hugging the far wall. More than twenty feet of space separated us from him, and for a moment he appeared to totter on the brink of tumbling into the emptiness.

His lesson went on, but encouraged by our accomplishments, we dared more. Jimmy Bufano led the way. In one fluid motion, it seemed, he left his desk and reappeared in the clothes closet near the classroom door. Next went Timothy O'Leary. Then Joseph Pagliari. Then another and another, until a full one-third of the class was laughing and elbowing each other in the increasingly narrow darkness of the closet, listening to the distant strains of Brother Placid's voice, "Milk cans . . . milk . . . pasteurized . . ."

Even when the light struck us like an Old Testament bolt of lightning, and we understood that the door had been flung open by the principal, we knew that the punishment would be worth the stories that we would be able to tell one another. We knew that it would be a story that would outlast Brother Placid's class and religion bees and spelling bees and history bees, a story that would go beyond the circles and rows that education set for us. We saw a new shape for our education. We saw that we could create our own stories out of this place, this school, and the Bronx itself.

There were things about the limits of the classroom that I loved. My desk was as familiar as my own hand. Lines carved into oak, faded ink stains, gashes, chips, depressions—the desk was a comforting, familiar landscape, connecting my life to all the other initials written in the dark wood. The classroom smelled of chalk, books, cleaning fluid, and damp coats. It smelled stale and sweet. When the windows were closed and everyone was silent, there was a tidal hum, which probably came from the lights, but then I thought it was the building itself, breathing and sighing. An American flag angled from the side of the room. A crucifix hung above the middle of the blackboard. Maps covered parts of the walls. A globe stood on a table near the teacher's desk, and next to it was a box of multicolored reading exercises. We marked our progress by the color of the passages we read. Each day we looked at the backs of the same heads, the hair wet combed or knotted by sleep. In the winter, the hiss of steam mixed with our recitations. In the late spring, the groans of buses on the street mingled with our whispered talk. We watched each other diagram sentences on the board, making phrases into strange branching rivers, pooled up into lines of prepositions and complements and adverbs. Words became physical objects—mysteries that could be viewed as they were placed in diagrams like trophies on shelves or that could be touched, tasted by the tongue, joined somehow into sentences and paragraphs and whole stories. Diagramming a sentence over and over again, spelling a word aloud until it felt like an ancient response, memorizing a poem for an oral test—all these made language seem incantatory. Words began to appear to be the most interesting game of all.

Sometime in the midst of elementary school I fell in love with books. It didn't matter if they were fact or fiction, as long as they had a sense of magic and a familiar remoteness to them. In games, I believe, most of us wanted to see ourselves as we thought our fathers once were—hopeful, passionate, and strong. In books, I listened for a father's voice—wise and compassionate, teasing and understanding.

In the fifth grade, my mother gave me a biography of Kit Carson. I read the book eight times in that school year and dreamed my way into each day and through history and math classes as Kit Carson. When the teacher asked me a question, I shook myself quickly out of my internal world, sometimes taking a second or two to realize that Mother David or Mrs. Murther was calling on me, *Kit Carson,* but using a name that I didn't recognize. Books became an escape from the present, in the classroom at St. Philip Neri or in the living room at home. Books were a way to forget the world, what Richard Wright called them, "a drug, a dope." And they were addictive. The more I read, the more I wanted to read. For me, Kit Carson *was* a pathfinder. He led me toward Don Quixote and David Copperfield, Pip and Tom Sawyer, the Joads and the Lilliputians. He also led me back to the world, to see how close I could bring my changing vision of possibility to the rigid nature of things. The stories I read made me feel as if I were threading a needle, squinting as I tried to find a way to angle my dreams through whatever aperture the world would allow.

I was fourteen years old when I found a used paperback copy of Herman Wouk's *Youngblood Hawke* in a bookstore on Fordham Road. It was Christmas vacation, but what I remember of that time has little to do with presents or holiday cheer. Instead, I remember reading about Youngblood Hawke, an untutored genius, a natural writer. I read his story in my bedroom until my eyes ached and burned, until the very air seemed to turn white. The book, 878 pages long, kept me in my room for days, except when I needed food or had to do something else. When I rearranged the shape of furious loneliness that my life often seemed to be and entered

Youngblood Hawke's story for hour after hour, day after day during that Christmas vacation, at first I saw only the romantic contours of the narrative. The novel fit the curve of my adolescent yearnings like a complementary puzzle piece. From Hovey, Kentucky, Hawke was, like me, a small-town boy (my neighborhood in the Bronx felt like a small town then), and *he* became an overnight success. Like my father, Hawke had been a Seabee, but unlike him, Hawke had not yielded his dreams to an indifferent world. The novel was the Horatio Alger tale, the perfect adolescent myth, retold by Wouk as the story of the rocketlike rise of an unkempt, gargantuan innocent who won the Pulitzer Prize. The picture on the cover of my frayed, water-stained Signet edition was of a shapely older woman, naked and in the embrace of a square-jawed young novelist. It was Hawke, but I wondered, "Couldn't it be me?"

Hawke was like a character in the *Arabian Nights*—a man who, according to Wouk, "wielded his gifts like a conquistador to re-enact the American dream." He had the confidence to escape his gloomy life in a coal-mining district of Kentucky, to leave behind an absent father and bleak skies. Arthur Hawke knew Hovey, Kentucky, "as a prisoner knows his cell," as I felt I knew the Bronx. And he left. He wrote books. He made a life from telling stories, from playing passionately with words.

When I recently reread *Youngblood Hawke,* I acknowledged what I suspected at fourteen. It is not a very good book, and Wouk is to be admired, as one critic said, "more for his stamina than his storytelling." But a voice in that book told me then to watch and wait; it suggested that living and creating are one and the same, that writing is an act of faith, that, perhaps, all real adventure begins in the imagination.

Books became a game for me. Words took the place of Spaldeens. I suspended disbelief, and the quality of the game and its outcome became a matter of true gravity. Literature, like the other games I played, was a matter of ultimate importance. Even then I knew, if you were not serious, why play at all?

Church was another sort of game. It had a language filled with secrets. Brother Placid had taught us that.

We knew that God made us "to know Him and to love Him and to serve Him." We learned the mystery of the Holy Trinity, the names of the sacraments, the place where the innocent babies go if they die before being baptized. School was an unending series of competitions—who had memorized the catechism best, which team answered the most questions in history and could therefore be dismissed first from class at the end of the day, who wore honor roll pins, who sat in the first row and who in the last. In many ways, it wasn't much different than the playground, than a game of Johnny-on-the-pony. It was the competition that they taught us, the necessary discipline to win, an affection for the rules of the game, a love of the game itself.

The rules associated with church were fairly simple. If you did not go to mass on Sunday, you had committed a mortal sin. If you died with a mortal sin on your soul, you went to hell, and that meant an eternity of burning lakes, unquenched thirst, unending screams, an eternity with demons who would look exactly like Brother Boniface. No matter how unfair we might have felt it would have been to end up with murderers and slave traders because we had skipped church and perhaps been struck down by a city bus as we headed for the park to play touch football, we knew that hell is where we would have ended up. So, throughout grade school, few of us dared to miss mass on Sunday. Our minds may have strayed during the service, but our bodies were there.

I remember often staring at the altar as the priest and altar boys drifted slowly into darkness, and I hypnotized myself on the words of the liturgy and a pinpoint of candlelight that I fixed my gaze upon. Everything would grow gray, then darker, then black, and the flame of the candle would shift from orange to red and finally become white. It felt like a religious experience to me, but I knew even then that it was a game in which I tested which parts of the world I could erase, if for only an instant. One at a time I blanked out a different part of the church, the pew in front of me, the congregation to my right and left, the steps leading to the altar, the priest, the chalice, everything but the light. Then I would see how long I could hold my vision as the shadows around the point of light tried to push their way back into the picture. I may have imagined that if I could hold this vision I would disappear into it, but I was always jolted back, and I never missed Holy Communion.

Church meant more than Sunday mass to us, for it became an inextricable part of each school day; crucifixes bobbed on nuns' gowns, rosary beads hung from brothers' pockets, and religion followed our every move. During Lent our lives were permeated by the spirit of Catholicism. We made our Lenten sacrifices. We ate no meat on Friday, and if we remembered this a few minutes after eating a White Castle hamburger, the meat became indigestible guilt, at least for a moment. Each Friday afternoon of Lent Brother Bruce took us to church to say the stations of the cross. We would sit in the semidarkness and say Hail Marys and Our Fathers while we glimpsed out of the corner of our eyes the various stations of the story of the crucifixion.

Each Friday after school during Lent we spent an hour in church saying the rosary to the stations of the cross. Once school was dismissed, Brother Bruce would lead a straggling, reluctant line of boys into the chapel. I know we dreamt of our freedom as we said our prayers. For forty days Lent stayed with us, and I'm sure most of us went through various stages of saintliness and disrespect throughout the years. At some point we may have even relished the challenge of giving up candy or ice cream for more than a month.

But by the seventh and eighth grades most of us had traded hopes of sainthood for dreams of a chance at the NFL or the NBA.

Sainthood was probably more feasible for many of us, but it had simply lost its attraction. So, each Friday afternoon as we squirmed on the wooden pews and knelt with our backsides slumped against the seats, we dreamt of deliverance. At times the prayers became mesmerizing. Brother Bruce's deep voice rose and fell: "Our Father, who art in heaven, hallowed be thy name. Thy kingdom come. Thy will be done, on earth as it is in heaven. Give us this day our daily bread. And forgive us our trespasses, as we forgive those who trespass against us. And lead us not into temptation . . ." Listening to his voice in the sunless church, many of us fell into something like an irreligious trance, dreaming of footballs arcing overhead and basketballs spinning toward a backboard.

But most often we sat there uncomfortably conscious that we were trapped. And we daydreamed about courses of rebellion. I often imagined myself standing up as Brother Bruce pronounced the last syllable of *temptation,* the *shun* echoing in everyone's ears as I walked up to him and said, matter-of-factly, "I have to leave now. I think God would rather see me playing football." Of course, I had very little idea what God wanted to see me doing, but I was pretty certain it wasn't playing football, and I never left my pew during those prayers. Along with the rest of my classmates, though, I did engage in my own forms of rebellion. When it came time for us to say the Hail Mary, I would move my lips but say no words or, better yet, the wrong ones. Brother Bruce would say, "Hail Mary, full of grace, the Lord is with thee. Blessed art thou among women and blessed is the fruit of thy womb, Jesus." But some of the others and I would chant, "Holy Mary, Mother of God . . . chase the chickens out of the yard . . . now and at the hour of our death. Amen." Many of us probably felt guilty at times for the sacrilege of saying such words in church, and most likely we regretted reciting any mocking phrases because we respected Brother Bruce for his kindness and strength. We said them anyway, one eye on Brother Bruce, the other on the altar. Besides, we were all city kids and a phrase like "chase the chickens out of the yard" seemed as harmless as cursing in French.

Most of us resigned ourselves to the stations of the cross each Friday of Lent as if we were Christian martyrs and it were our destiny to view the fourteen scenes representing Christ's passion and death. At St. Philip's Church the stations were depicted on the stained-glass windows that lined each of the walls leading to the altar. When I wasn't mouthing blasphemous words or dreaming of being elsewhere, I often fell fully into the narrative the stations outlined. I saw Pilate condemning Christ, and as the Hail Marys and Our Fathers buzzed around the room, I dreamt of unheroic Pilate, washing his hands of things, wanting to be neither guilty nor courageous. I imagined Christ's falls and his meetings with his mother and Veronica. I heard the noisy streets and the sound of his garments being torn from him, the shouts of the crowds, and I breathed in the acrid smell of despair. In the back of my mind, perhaps, was the knowledge that the story led toward Easter and redemption and a new suit of clothes, but as the story pulled me forward, it seemed to steer me toward a contemplation of those individual faces in the mob, those ordinary souls lost in the crowds that stood invisible, an implication outside the frame of the stained-glass parable.

And one Friday afternoon, as I dreamt of particular faces blurred in a moving crowd, one face cut free from the pack: Jimmy Bufano's. Actually, it was the back of his head that I saw as it slid slowly from sight two pews in front of me. The top of his dirty blond hair disappeared, and the boys in his aisle nudged one another and turned their heads to follow his long, skinny form snaking along the narrow kneeling stool. He made it to the far end of the pew and crept along the wall under the last seven stations of the cross. At one point Brother Bruce looked back at our group, but by that time the boys had shifted to close up the space left by

Jimmy. Just as Brother Bruce stood up and walked back along the rows, Jimmy crawled into the empty confessional. Any of us who saw him gently close the confessional door must have pondered the audacity of the violation and probably cheered the undaunted courage it took to enter that dark booth to hide.

The only times I had entered the confessional booth had been to wait for the priest to slide the window-sized screen open to reveal a bored, silhouetted profile ready to listen to my modest sins. "Bless me, Father, for I have sinned . . . it has been one month since my last confession." Always, the sexual sins were placed neatly between moments of disrespect and laziness. I suppose I hoped that the priest would not hear what I considered to be the real sins when they were hidden between such mundane crimes of the spirit. But perhaps his exhausted expression was in response to all my sins, especially the sexual ones, which were, in retrospect, the dullest of my transgressions.

The confessional was a sacred place to most of us. The secrets passed from sinner to priest were private, and as much as I yearned to hear clearly the muffled conversation on the other side of the booth, I knew it was a sin to listen. The confessional was solemn. You knelt there in total darkness until the priest opened the screen and became a shadow and a soft voice. In the booth you could tell only the truth, and the priest, speaking for God, would grant you forgiveness. You left the confessional unburdened, as if you had just shaken off dirt from the grave. Five Hail Marys and five Our Fathers, and you started again with a clear conscience.

For most of us, crawling into the confessional to hide would have been like slipping into an upright coffin. I had the sense that such things didn't bother Jimmy Bufano, though. I imagined his glinting smile in the musty darkness. I could almost see him leaning back in against the screen as Brother Bruce walked by and as "Holy Mary, mother of God, chase the chickens out of the yard" came to him like the slurred syllables of a prisoners' chant. When Brother Bruce passed by the confessional, the door opened a crack, and I watched Bufano's dark gaze follow him back to his seat. Then the door opened, and he crouched down and vanished without another sound, past the holy water and the organ pipes, as if he had ascended into heaven.

However, he did not go any farther than two blocks away to Villa Avenue, and by the following Monday he was back in school with the rest of us. Of course, he was not like the rest of us anymore. He had come close to ascending into heaven. He had escaped the stations of the cross, he had disappeared, become spirit when the rest of us were trapped in flesh; he had performed a miracle, and none of us would soon forget that. I'm not sure if he ever again made a similar exit or if any of us did, but somehow it didn't matter because we knew that he had once, that one of us had once, which was enough to change the rules of the game.

It was Jimmy Bufano, with his scimitar-shaped smile, who pushed me into my last fight. Fights were the ultimate game, full of complicated rules that had to be observed. Of course, Jimmy was a master fighter. He was a year older than most of us, sinewy and tall. And fearless. He would fight anyone . . . and he often did, for no apparent reason. His irrationality, his simple craziness, made him feared. But as wild as he was, there was nothing malicious about him, nothing of the bully. He just seemed to enjoy fighting. It brought a smile to his face. He even enjoyed other people's fights.

We were in the eighth grade. It was toward the end of a dull week, and Jimmy seemed desperate for some stimulation. The knife edges of his smile curved up when he saw me walking out of the lunch room behind Gary Delano. I hated Gary Delano. I may be mistaken now, but it seemed to me then that everybody did. He had an unctuous laugh that was somehow self-righteous and lurid at the same time. And, unlike Jimmy, Gary was a bully, always picking on the ghostly Tommy Murray or the waiflike Tony Mahoney. So I disliked him—the sound of his voice, his superior smile, his greasy black hair. But I had no desire to fight him, for he was taller and heavier than I was. Nearly everyone in the class was. I was still waiting to break one hundred pounds, and Gary Delano looked as if he ate half that much for lunch.

Fate, assisted by Jimmy Bufano, gave me no choice that day— or, at least, at thirteen years old, I felt that I had no choice but to fight Gary Delano. As I walked out of the lunchroom, Jimmy Bufano pushed me into Delano's back, knocking his tray into his stomach, spilling the remains of his container of milk all over his already stained white shirt. He immediately dropped the tray and turned around, shoving me into the wall. Bufano, smiling, stepped between us and said, "C'mon you two, let's take it into the bathroom."

The last time I had fought with a Villa Avenue boy I was in the fourth grade, and it had not been a great success. I had been in the Italian neighborhood, visiting my bespectacled friend Martin St. John, when a swaggering kid everyone called Little Man approached us. Marty may have had a scholarly appearance, but he was Italian, and he was from Villa Avenue. I was neither, which made me ripe for an attack from Little Man. He probably wasn't much older than I was, but he already had the beginnings of a moustache, and he seemed determined to live up to his Homeric nickname and to use me as one more anecdote for his legend. He started a fight, and we rolled around the curb and under the tailpipes of a few parked cars. I'm fairly certain that I was actually winning until the crowd grew and the circle of dark-haired boys began to chant, "Get him, Little Man." My strength and courage disappeared when I began to think about the fact that I had a headlock on a mustachioed little man. He seemed to sense his advantage immediately, and I soon found my arms pinned against the street by his knees and heard my humiliating response to his smirking question, "Yeah, I give up."

Gary Delano reminded me of Little Man, only a little less hairy. By the time we got into the bathroom and removed our school jackets, a crowd had gathered and encircled us, blocking the stalls and the urinals, giving us no place to escape. Some of my friends and some of his were in that circle, but I remember only one face vividly. On the outer edge of the circle by the bathroom door, Rudy Figuera stood with his wide eyes and vacant smile. I remember glimpsing Rudy's gnomelike face, wondering how I ended up in the bathroom facing Delano, and wishing someone bigger was getting ready to smash his self-satisfied grin.

He took a swing that missed my head and caught the edge of my shoulder blade, and there was no more time to ponder ill fortune. I just sidestepped and swung, catching him with a lucky punch that struck the side of his face. The punch scared me because I thought it would infuriate him so that he would charge like a maddened animal, but instead it wiped the smug grin from his face and made him more tentative. That's when we started the circling ritual that usually began such moments. We angled and shoved— hearts beating fast, mouths drying up, and both of us, I'm sure, praying for the bell to call us back to class. At one point, Bufano, bored with the way things were heading, pushed Delano into me, and we fell onto the cold tile floor, which was damp and smelled of urine mixed with disinfectant. We struggled to our feet, pulled each other's ties, gave short jabs to the stomach, and tried unsuccessfully to hit each other's faces.

Again we began to circle, but although my eyes were fixed on Delano's, I was thinking about Patty Dougherty and a fight we had had in the summer after the seventh grade. As with most of the fights my friends and I engaged in, this one started with words. When we spoke to one another, we had only two tones, it seemed— ironic and brutally ironic. For us, words were a vehicle for not saying what we really meant. Our conversations were a strange version of pig Latin, where everything we said meant something else, most often its opposite. Fighting indicated the failure of irony, I suppose. Our language simply couldn't keep up with our emotions. As with Billy Budd, the words stuttered, collapsed, and locked in our muscles. Usually in those circumstances we punched someone in the face.

So I circled warily, watching Delano and thinking of Patty and me on 198th Street across the Concourse from my apartment. It was late afternoon, and we struck each other hard, knocking against parked cars that felt warm in the fading sunlight. Patty slipped, and I landed on top of him in a perfect position to sit on his chest and swing my fists in a wild windmill against his face. I swung a few times and then was jerked backward as if I had been snatched away in a dream. It was my father—who had watched the fight develop from our kitchen window and walked across the wide boulevard—placing one hand roughly against Patty's face and the other on my collar, pushing him down with a thud and snapping me up with a click of air into my lungs.

At the time I felt a deep surge of embarrassment that my father would intervene, but years later I remembered his actions as a suggestion of his love. He had watched me, then, I thought, and he had stepped into my life. As I eyed Gary Delano, I wished for him to be there again. But before it was all over, Gary and I rose from the ammonia-scented tile floor and got back on our feet, landing a few more punches. He hit me once solidly on the ear, and I felt my knuckles land squarely on his nose, hearing a crack but being unable to tell if it came from his face or my hand. The bell rang while we were still angling for a new position, nobody the clear winner, but Jimmy Bufano smiling at the time well spent in something like a joust before English and geography lessons. He smiled as if to say, "This is better than diagramming sentences."

We tucked our shirts in, straightened our ties, and marched back into the classroom for a different sort of game. One more spelling bee. Another circle. I lasted longer than Gary Delano.

Jimmy Bufano fell even before Gary. Brother Placid's voice drifted over the transom from the room across the hall, blurred syllables all running into one another, "homogenized . . . sterilized . . . milk . . . milk." And Rudy Figuera remained standing at the end, knowing something the rest of us didn't, but never saying what that was, just smiling like an Italian American Buddha and spelling all the words correctly, always spelling the words exactly right.

.....

St. Philip Neri Church and Elementary School match my memory of them, unfaded by thirty years. The last time I walked into the school building was November 22, 1963. I had the day off from Mount St. Michael High School, where I was a freshman, and I had come back to tell Brother Bruce that the president had been shot. I have never returned until now.

The past is alive in this school building. For a moment it seems as if time has stood perfectly still. I wouldn't be too surprised to see Gary Delano turn the corner, hands on his hips, ready to commence the fight again, or Mary Cunyon stroll down the hall, a wicked smile on her face as she brushes against my hip on her way to the main office. If I peek into one of the classrooms, I might find myself like Woody Allen in *Annie Hall,* looking back at himself as he reentered his past. There would be a circle of faces: Benny Ianello, now a smugly successful building contractor; Tommy Murray, even more pallid after years in the navy that seemed more miserable than those in elementary school; Jimmy Bufano, still a willowy teenager because, perhaps like Huck Finn, he had no other choice but to remain the same or to disappear entirely. I stand there, not breathing too hard, afraid that the slightest move or inhalation will break the spell and the dream will slip away. I step forward, breathe deeply, but surprisingly the world stays in place. The gymnasium has the same narrow slats of wood, the stained white backboards, the frosted glass windows, the stage, the balcony seats. I jumped onto that stage a hundred times to retrieve basketballs that had bounced out of someone's reach. The floor appears to sag in precisely the same spots it had once sagged. As I stand there remembering errant passes and school assemblies, two eighth-grade boys come into the gym bouncing a ball. They appear to be Hispanic, but they could be Italian, and this could be 1962: their green ties read SPN, their white shirts are untucked, their ties askew, their hair rumpled.

Outside the gym, in the classroom corridor on the first floor, is a showcase built into the cement-block wall. The showcase no longer has glass doors as it once had, but the walls are still painted green and white. I remember sliding my fingers along the grouted lines as I took a sidelong glance at my composition framed behind the glass. I wanted to stare at it there, my words held out for all to read, but I didn't want anyone to suspect I cared about such things.

"Michael, slow down," a voice calls in a soft but authoritative brogue, and I look up guiltily, caught speeding back into my own past. The voice belongs to Brother Brian Johnson, the principal of St. Philip's, but the Michael he is calling to is a third grader on his way to the lunchroom in the basement. A bit later, as Brother Brian and I walk down to the cafeteria, he stops to speak with a plumber about "flushometers," to answer a seventh-grade boy's question about basketball practice, and to pick a stray candy wrapper from the floor.

In the lunchroom, the children sit at long tables, eighth graders at one, second graders at another. Milk containers spill over the sides of brown plastic garbage bags at the entranceway, and Brother Brian stops to pick up the few that have landed on the floor. He says hello to each of the lunchroom ladies and talks briefly with the assistant principal. Brother Brian, a Franciscan, and one nun are the only religious teachers in the school. Thirty years ago there were no full-time lay teachers.

As I watch him move between the tables, speak with older students, help third graders with their trays, straighten a tie, pat a head, I realize that much of what I cherished about St. Philip's was personified by men like Brother Bruce and Brother Gwyn or women like Sister Annunciata and even Mother Concepta. As they once were, Brother Brian is the heart of this school.

He has been at St. Philip's as its principal since 1981. He is in his forties, balding and sports something akin to a Van Dyke beard, but he has an unshorn, elfin look, wide eyed, with a friendly, crooked-toothed grin and a scop's lyrical voice.

He grew up in the west of Ireland in County Galway near the banks of the Shannon and attended Galway University for one year before coming to the United States. After two years at Loyola Marymount in Los Angeles, he went to teach at Cardinal Hayes High School in the South Bronx, where he worked for the next twelve years while he finished his degree at St. Francis College in Brooklyn.

We walk toward his office near the entranceway to the school, and we stop for a moment as he bends down to speak with a small boy who holds a carton of frozen milk against his sore foot. Brother Brian's office is crammed with his thirteen years as principal—a boomerang, photographs of the old country and of friends from the new one, a miniature backboard and hoop, plaques, letters, a teddy bear next to a picture of Pope Paul. The plaque, given to him in Ireland in 1988, reads: "To Brother Brian Johnson for 25 years of dedicated service to the order of St. Francis." The teddy bear comes with a letter from Jasmine, one of his students a few years ago: "Thank you and Mr. Bear for helping me feel better and happier." Brother Brian had given her the bear to hold onto, to comfort her, when she found out her father had been shot.

In the eight years I spent at St. Philip's as a child I cannot recall one story of such violence, but Brother Brian can recount many:

Michael Clark, a seventh grader, shot and killed last year; a boy's father, who was a postal worker, shot; another child, whose father was a police officer, gunned down. "Every Monday," Brother Brian tells me, "we pray for all those who died over the weekend, especially at the hands of violent people." Years ago St. Philip's was merely a part of the world in the Bronx, an extension of family and neighborhoods, but now it seems a haven from much of what surrounds it. Brother Brian, glancing down at Jasmine's letter, tries to explain it, as much to himself as to me: "It's simply a far more violent place. There's more money, so it's not poverty. I think it's drugs and indifference. Those violent kids have no sense of belonging. Schools like this have to be kept intact for the kids' sake. They need a place away from the world, where they are secure, cared for, taught."

During our conversation the phone rings twice, and I read a collection of notes written to me by the two eighth-grade classes I spoke to earlier in the day. One in particular stands out, seems to sum up the sixty notes I received. This one, from Jennel Williams, says:

> Thirty years from now I see myself with a nice husband and lots of lovely children. I want maybe six kids, because I love them so much, they make a room light up. I'm not sure what profession I want, but when the time comes I'll be decided. I don't see myself in the Bronx, to me it's a hell-hole. I've seen people get shot and killed. I even seen my own seventeen-year-old brother get shot. I was in a hit and run accident and was in the hospital for a week. I don't want to be too negative about the Bronx, the pizza is not so bad.

In her letter, in most of the letters, there is a thread of light in the midst of the dark reality—as well as, finally, a sense of humor. Most of these students seem to realize that the Bronx is a place for survivors, a place that teaches you how to survive.

As I read the letters, Brother Brian's telephone conversation cuts into my thoughts: "That's lovely. . . . Sure, that's fine. . . . God bless you." Then there is one more interruption as the secretary, a small dark-haired woman in red pants, red shoes, and a blue, yellow, and red blouse—more color than I can recall on any adult during my years as a student here—comes into the office to make photocopies of some custody papers. Briefly, in whispers, she discusses the situation with Brother Brian, who asks, "Is he sober or is he drunk or anything?" He leans on the copy machine, his head nearly touching the large crucifix that hangs on the wall behind it. "Just tell him we don't know anything," he says, but I sense he does. The situation is not that unusual, he tells me: a father who used drugs and alcohol and was abusive wants custody of his two children. The mother has taken the children and is in hiding. The school is legally in the middle, but the moral issue seems clear to Brother Brian, and he will do what he must to protect the children.

He walks over to the intercom and says, "Please stand for our final prayer. . . . In the name of the Father, Son, and the Holy Spirit, Amen. O my God, I am heartily sorry for having offended you, and I detest all my sins because of Your just punishments, but most of all because they offended You, my God, who are all good and deserving of all my love. I firmly resolve, with the help of Your goodness, to sin no more and to avoid the near occasions of sin."

I recall in a flash all those years trying unsuccessfully to avoid the occasions of sin, but I also recall those voices—Brother Bruce's or Brother Gwyn's—that were soft and gentle, like Brother Brian's, filled with understanding and forgiveness, not fire and brimstone. The younger children begin to line up in the hall. The parents gather in front of the school. The children are smiling, tugging at one another, eager to step into the cold. Snowball fights, not the final prayer, are in their eyes, and Brother Brian seems to sense that as he smiles back at them and sends them off with a word or wave of his hand.

A few minutes later, as he walks me toward the back exit, Brother Brian is stopped by a fifth-grade girl, who smooths her plaid skirt and asks, "Can I let the girls in now, Brother?" He looks at her with a dramatic seriousness, "You mean, 'may I?' Go ahead." We take a few steps, and a third-grade boy asks, "Should I clean up the hall now, Brother Brian?" Gently, he takes the boy's hands out of his pockets, saying, "Yes, Richard. Go ahead." Now, we are down the steps and we come across another young man. Brother Brian asks him if he still has detention. "I'm on *eternal* detention," the boy says and goes up the steps. Brother Brian lets out a magnificent laugh, and I suspect the boy has unwittingly won himself amnesty.

On the radio, WFUV, the public station broadcast from Fordham University, Carole King sings, "Sometimes I wonder if I'm ever gonna make it home again. It seems so far and out of sight." But, as much as I understand her feelings, I continue driving toward my old high school, Mount St. Michael, and when I see it on Nereid Avenue, in the midst of the two-family homes and narrow strips of lawn, I am back home again. I am fifteen years old in Mr. Tricario's social studies class, being teased by him and loving it. I am in Brother Eugene's English class, standing at my desk, reciting Portia's "The quality of mercy is not strained" speech from *The Merchant of Venice*. I am seventeen, keeping a wary eye out for Brother Charles Patrick, the dean of discipline. I am sixteen, in the quadrangle outside the cafeteria, listening to a group of seniors talk about their Spanish teacher, Brother Emiliano, also my instructor. They describe a hockey game field trip that he chaperoned—how they generously explained the American game to him (he was from South America), making it clear that it was tradition to scream "hit the fuck" at every opportunity. When he heard people in the crowd yelling "Hit the puck," he joined in with his own newly learned phrase. Even hockey fans can be surprised, it seems, at a cleric screaming obscenities. Eventually word got back to the school, and the boys had to explain their translating skills to Charley Patrick.

If anything, the school is bigger than I remember it. It takes up a full square block with a number of buildings, some of which were once dormitories when it was a boarding school. The main building has brick towers, an arched driveway that leads to a statue of the Archangel Michael slaying Satan. Beneath it is the motto, "Ad Astra per Aspera." The sky is already dark, but a straggling line of young men comes jogging back into the school, a few squares of light remain in the classroom windows, and the day seems far from over.

The local news is now on the radio: "An argument between two fourteen year olds after school today resulted in one hitting the other with a meat cleaver. The boy who was struck is in serious condition." When I click the radio off, I see the old Bronx, my friends and me at fourteen and fifteen, freshmen in high school, at our first dances, standing shyly along the walls, staring doe-eyed at the girls on the other side of the gymnasium, waiting desperately for a slow song and an encouraging look.

By the time I reach Dominick's Restaurant on Arthur Avenue in the Bronx, it is 6:30 and a light snowfall has already begun to sprinkle white against the darkness. The sound of distant carousel music mixes with the smell of fish from Cosenza's Store. Grey-haired women maneuver laundry carts from Calabria's Pork Store to Addeo's Bakery. Six friends, some whom I haven't seen for twenty years, show up to sit at one of the long wooden tables, drink red wine, eat pasta, and reminisce. Before we know it, it is past midnight, and four Italian waiters lean on chairs, staring in our direction, barely able to mask looks of frustration.

The stories, in a race with time, have won. Time, for a few hours, disappears. None of us hears a tick of the clock until the waiter steps in with a check. Al Arater, Chris Young, Frankie Bartoletti, Steve Tarnok, Dennis Murphy, and Robbie McDougal pass the stories back and forth. Stories of Rheinhold Steindorfer and Tony Mahoney. Stories of Bobby Maloney and Dennis Suane. Tales of Rip, of Brother Placid and Brother Bruce. Tribal memories. Stories of lost comrades, comedies of failure, sexual intrigue.

Dennis tells a story about Nicky Purillo, nicknamed "the Tool" for his legendary eighteen-inch member, and his introduction to a reputedly insatiable young woman named Barbara. Patty Dougherty introduced them by saying to Barbara, "This is Nicky. Pilgrim, your search has ended." Then, it seems, just about every-one at the table has a story in which Barbara is a supporting actress. Steve tells a story about Mrs. Murphy bustling around the kitchen and living room as Dennis hides Barbara in his bedroom the morn-ing after he snuck her into his mother's apartment. Al tells the story of how one night in Darby O'Gill's Dennis borrowed the keys to Rip's car and made himself comfortable with Barbara in the back seat. Al's mother stopped in at the bar, asked if she could get a ride with Rip, and told someone she would wait in his car. When she opened the door, saw the unclothed young woman, and caught a glimpse of the young man in the shadows, she asked, "Michael Toombs, is that you?" Dennis cleared his throat and said in his soft-est voice, "Yes, Mrs. Arater, it's me." Dennis laughs the loudest at that story, but we're all holding our sides when Al says, "It took Mike Toombs a year before he had the courage to come into my house again."

The stories are a bright flash that holds us all in the same light— stories of ill-fated trips to Jones' Beach, tales of Maud and Frankie naked on the roof of a summer rental in the Hamptons, stories of setting the seat of my then brand new 1966 Pontiac on fire with a marijuana cigarette and putting it out with a can of beer. It is Chris who remembers the three guys in the back seat arguing over who would have to give up his beer to be used as a fire extinguisher.

The years have passed. The pot bellies, bald spots, gray hairs, the glasses tell us so. But for five hours we master time with our stories. Once again we are kids in the Bronx. As we head out into the night, the waiters sighing with relief behind us, the darkness holds for me the same mystery that it did in childhood, and the snow that falls more heavily now seems to fall over the entire Bronx, the past and present alike.

CHAPTER 4

Girls

> *Lolita, my twin, was born decades later, yet twin of*
> *the thirteen-and-a-half-year-old striding through*
> *Crotona Park, passing the spiky red flowers through*
> *a kingdom of mesmerized men—young, old, skinny,*
> *fat, good-looking, well dressed, shabby, bachelors,*
> *fathers—all her subjects.*
>
> —Kate Simon, *Bronx Primitive*

> *What are little girls made of?*
>
> —Anonymous, nursery rhyme

The first time I saw Mary Cunyon I fell in love with her achingly and at a distance of one hundred yards. I was playing football in Van Cortlandt Park. We were backed up against our goal line, and she kicked her muscular legs into the air with a group of cheerleaders at the other end of the field. I believe I was in the sixth grade, but I know for certain that the air felt brittle and the sky was pewter. It was the kind of day that made you want to stay out until the sky turned a dark blue and your face and hands tingled with cold and the anticipation of a warm house.

I usually played defense, but I was fast and dreamed of carrying the ball. This was the first time that I got my chance. The quar-

109

terback called a running play for me. As he shouted the signals, everything seemed to slow down to a speed that allowed me to feel like a spectator rather than a player. The quarterback took the snap and pivoted to the left. I slanted from my halfback position and took the handoff about three yards behind the line of scrimmage. I remember seeing the gaping hole that our offensive line had created. The space seemed to be five yards wide, and nothing blocked my view of the goal posts and Mary Cunyon, who stood behind them.

I recall quite clearly her short brown hair blowing in the wind as the earth tilted and she seemed to stand on her head. But, of course, she never moved. It was I who tripped over my own feet as I sliced into the wide, heroic spaces before me and fell thunderously onto one of the patches of grass on the dusty field.

I played defense for the rest of my short career, and for a time after that I avoided Mary Cunyon's eyes in the schoolyard. But for some reason she seemed to have an interest in me. It was, perhaps, the first in a long line of surprises that girls had in store for me. My relationship with Mary Cunyon was more short-lived than my football career, which lasted through a few seasons of Pop Warner, but it had its highlights. In those subtle ways a preteen girl lets a boy know she is interested in him—through emissaries, shy smiles, and anonymous notes—Mary Cunyon communicated with me, and one day we found ourselves walking home together from Van Cortlandt Park. Along the way we kissed—sixty-three times, for we counted those kisses. Probably realizing that we had no hope of attaining quality, we reached for quantity instead and what we may have thought was some sort of local record for a fall afternoon in our neighborhood. I was happy to be the object of her affections but confused by her interest. Hadn't she seen my humiliating stumble?

That stroll with Mary Cunyon was my first clue that girls might be interested in different things than boys, that they might see value in things that I had not recognized. I suspected that the mothering instinct might extend to dating, that a boy like me, shy and stumbling, might very well be viewed as a raw lump of clay, ready to be molded by the right person into various shapes of perfection. Boys, I believe, had a different attitude. We had no desire to transform someone. We wanted them to be perfect already. Up to that point my contact with girls had been minimal—my older sister, Virginia, her friends, a blur of plaid skirts and white blouses in school. A few years before, Sheila—an older girl who lived next door and who had, for me, the exotic quality of being Jewish—invited me into her home to play post office. The menorah replacing the crucifix that I was used to seeing, her apartment had a strangeness that I associated with her tight-lipped kisses.

After my kissing record with Mary Cunyon, which was disputed by Bobby Maloney, who said they had kissed seventy times in one afternoon, I didn't have much to do with girls until the seventh grade, when I met Angela Sorrentino. She was half Italian, but she didn't live in one of those disheveled, mysterious three-family houses on Villa Avenue. She lived in a fancy place on Briggs Avenue, the sort of apartment building that once had a doorman or at least always looked as if it should have had one.

Angela was an odd balance of saint and siren. With her tight brown curls and her plump face and pudgy legs, she might have been the picture of a young nun. She attended church regularly. On Palm Sunday she carried home more than her share of golden, feather-shaped leaves to design into crosses for her bookshelves and dresser tops. On Easter she wore frilly dresses and implausible hats. On Ash Wednesday her forehead looked like a chimney sweep's. During Lent she went to mass each Friday morning before school. She was simply holier than anyone besides the nuns and older Irish and Italian women who waddled sadly into the church every morning of the year, blessing themselves with the holy water and wearily genuflecting before the main altar. But Angela had a coquettish smile and the inclination to rub up against you even when there was plenty of open space. She would come out of early morning mass during the week and walk up to me in the playground, gently brush against my hip as she asked if I had seen Mother David. When we were sitting down, she had the habit of resting her hand on my leg as she talked about the research she did for her report on Philip Neri, the saint whose name adorned the front of the school building. She got a fervent look on her face and squeezed my thigh a few times as she talked about St. Philip's ascetic life in Renaissance Italy. Philip, who died in 1595, a few months before his eightieth birthday, seemed alive to her. She spoke about him as if he had been the principal of the school. She loved the idea that he had left his formal study to speak directly with the people in hospitals and marketplaces. Her goal, she told me with a slight pressure on my knee, was to become a candy striper.

Somewhere along the way, Angela's fervent looks scared me. Or perhaps it was the presents she bought me for birthdays and holidays. She could afford them, but the gift wrapping and the talk of Philip Neri in Campo were enough to unbalance me. Once we went out to eat at a diner near Villa Avenue, but she would only have a soda. "I'll watch you eat," she said and rubbed her leg against mine. It wasn't until years later that I wondered if she refused to eat because it wasn't sexy or because it was too much so. Was she afraid of getting lettuce stuck in her teeth, or had she paid careful attention to the nuns' warnings that if girls ordered ravioli on a date, their boyfriends might think about pillows? About the time I started to imagine her in twenty years in the accoutrement of a Sister of the Sacred Heart but with a slit up the side of the robe and a lacy black negligee underneath, I renewed my interest in baseball, and she went to church even more frequently.

Not long after that, I met Elka. She was slim and tall and Lutheran. All of those things made her appealing. She wasn't beautiful, but she had the kind of Germanic face that seemed to be able to transform itself on occasion. In the morning she might have looked like a Bulgarian peasant woman, but by that very same afternoon she was exotic and aristocratic. In the moonlight she could turn into a Tess of the D'Urbervilles, all wide-eyed and wildly innocent. At night her hint of a Slavic accent, which in the daylight embarrassed me and seemed to shame her into silence, was full of romantic promise. I had to stand on my tiptoes to kiss her, but it was worth the awkwardness. At Jimmy Durella's birthday party I played "Seven Minutes in Heaven" with her, Jimmy turning out all the living room lights when his mother was next door visiting a neighbor. Sitting on one of Mrs. Durella's sofas next to Elka, I forgot about our difference in height and her strange accent. We concentrated on making our lips fit together perfectly until Mrs. Durella stormed back into the unlit room and played careful chaperon for the rest of the evening.

At Tommy Slater's house a few months later, Elka and I somehow made our way into his parents' bedroom and lay down on the bed. I'm not sure which one of us suggested the move to the bedroom, but I remember pressing my body against hers, her mouth softening and opening against mine in a way it hadn't at Jimmy Durella's. In between those meetings at rare parties or brief encounters near Mosholu Park, Elka and I never saw one another. She went to public school and lived in the basement of an apartment building on Briggs Avenue. Simply being a girl made her a strange creature to me, but living beneath the ground made her seem alien and otherworldly. Besides, back then all the boys I knew had the same idea about dating—see a girl once or twice a month on the benches near the park and never speak to her otherwise.

On moist summer evenings Elka and I might move into the shadows, away from the others who leaned against the black metal fence, and she would turn her head toward mine. I would glance at the portion of sky visible through a break of trees along the parkway and see the pattern of lights in the blue blackness of night. The geometry of the stars, the Big Dipper or Gemini, would hold like a flash of afterlight in my mind as I closed my eyes and she slid her tongue into my mouth.

Then there was confession on Saturday afternoon. "Bless me, Father, for I have sinned. I was selfish . . . disobedient . . . impure in thought and deed. . . . I was disrespectful. . . ." The dark profile of the priest's head would turn almost imperceptibly, and he would ask, "These impure deeds, my son, were they done alone or with others?" For an instant, I would imagine an orgy, me and a half-dozen Elkas in Tommy Slater's parents' bedroom. Another impure thought, one that would have to wait for the next confession. My sins could be produced, I realized, almost too quickly for God's emissary to forgive them. My answer to the priest's question was always the same: "Both, father." And, somehow, I always felt more shame for my lonely sins, sensing that the failure was not merely religious, but social too. It didn't seem as bad to sin if someone else thought you attractive enough to be drawn toward you.

I envied Elka, for she didn't have to confess her sins. We never spoke of such things, but probably for her they weren't sins. They didn't feel like sins to me either, but for some reason it felt good to walk out of the fractured light of the church into the afternoon sun with an unblemished soul, ready to be saintly, but knowing deep down inside that I wouldn't and would be forgiven for it anyway.

Somewhere along the way Elka disappeared from my life. I don't remember if she got tired of me or I of her. Perhaps one of those breaks between parties or gaps between meetings along the fence railing of Mosholu Park turned into a long enough stretch to make us forget about each other or merely become interested in something else—a new bike or another sports season. Whatever happened, just as Angela seemed to drift away down the vestibule of the church, Elka vanished into the smell of coal and refuse underground.

Ginger lived two stories above the ground, and she may have been my first girlfriend. If my memory is accurate, we began going out toward the end of eighth grade or the summer before high school. It lasted a long time by a teenager's standard—until the end of my freshman year in high school. I thought she looked like Natalie Wood, but really all they had in common was dark brown hair. However, I was willing to think Ginger resembled Natalie Wood for a number of reasons. First, I loved Natalie Wood because she was beautiful, but also because she seemed so vulnerable as she read lines from Wordsworth's "Ode: Intimations of Immortality" in the movie *Splendor in the Grass:*

> What though the radiance which was once so bright
> Be now forever taken from my sight,
>   Though nothing can bring back the hour
> Of splendor in the grass, of glory in the flower;
>   We will grieve not, rather find
>   Strength in what remains behind.

I had not lived enough to understand what Wordsworth meant by the "philosophic mind" or by "what remains behind," but I saw Natalie Wood's beauty and sorrow, and I was ready to believe that Ginger had both. I also liked the name *Ginger.* It was the spicy sound, I suppose. Plus, she was slim, and people called her "cute." Most important, though, she was shorter than I was. When you are in the eighth grade and only five feet tall, it's not easy to find a girl who doesn't tower over you. So Ginger was Natalie Wood as far as I was concerned.

We dated for about a year. That is, we pressed our bodies together like playful seals—in her hallway, against the railings in the park, in her living room, in the movie theater. Always with all of our clothes on, we bumped and grinded as if we had been asked to simulate adult sex. In the calculated manner of a thirteen-year-old Catholic schoolgirl, she was passionate. When I left her house, my shirt was always untucked.

One summer afternoon at the P.S. 8 Recreation Center, we played strip poker. Not much clothing came off, but it was an exciting afternoon anyway because it was filled with implication, the possibility of nakedness. She was teasing; her looks were womanly and seductive, even if her chest was as flat as mine. When she laughed, a competitive half-smile creased her lips, a look I associated with boys, at once challenging and sarcastic and playful. She still had something of the tomboy about her. It had been only a few months before that that the older boys had made a habit of snapping the back of her bra through her blouses and asking her where her undershirt was. She had learned how to smack away their hands and say, "I lent it to your mother."

Soon, though, it wasn't necessary to come up with sarcastic responses. The older boys were interested in her and a different sort of teasing. Around that time, she lost some of her interest in me, I think. About a month after I bought her an ankle bracelet for her birthday, she told me she had a new boyfriend, a sophomore in high school. I'm sure that I was hurt, but in retrospect I believe I relished the *idea* of a broken heart and how much older it made me feel.

I always wanted to be older, to grow up faster. Girls, even when they were a bit younger than I was, always seemed older to me. Unlike boys, who seemed easy enough to read, girls were a hieroglyphic. They always wore hats in church, and if they didn't have hats, they pinned a handkerchief to their heads. I was never really sure why they had to cover their heads in church, but there were rumors about angels being tempted by beautiful hair. But if angels could be tempted by such things, what chance did I have? There was always something thrilling about teasing girls—stealing their hats in the schoolyard or pulling their hair in the classroom. Boys could scare you or make you angry or get you to laugh, but girls could make your heart race by just looking over in your direction. Girls seemed to have a secret language. They stood in circles and whispered. They laughed about matters that I didn't understand. They knew something that I didn't.

In the early sixties, girls and boys alike faced many of the same monsters—blobs and body snatchers, communists and fluoridation, blindness from masturbation or the blinding finale of the bomb. We were the first generation seriously to contemplate the end of the world as a scientific probability, not just as a religious prophecy. Girls during those years, like boys, faced the specter of the end of the world, but they faced other phantoms as well. The fifties sputtered to an end with the hula hoop and Bobby Darin and Paul Anka. By the early sixties I'm sure most of the girls were as confused as the boys were. Maybe some of them carried around a folded copy of Kennedy's inaugural address as I did—with the lines "ask not what your country can do for you" plainly visible. They, too, had most likely fallen in love with Jack and Jackie. Our parents had elected him, but we could look up to him, trust him. So this was what the future might hold for us: grace and beauty, success, a happy marriage. If we boys imagined ourselves as John Kennedy, tall and handsome, did the girls see themselves, in their pill box hats, as Jacqueline?

By the middle of the decade I suspect that many of those girls felt caught between two worlds, between the image of Sandra Dee from the 1950s and the one of Janis Joplin from the 1960s. Perhaps some of them still saw themselves as Jennifer Jones in *The Song of Bernadette*. They were different from us, separated from the rest of the world. Although in our college years most of us—both male and female—complained about the puritanical injustice of being separated throughout much of grade school and all of high school, I think many of the girls actually were relieved by the isolation. At such schools, Mary Gordon points out, it was all girls taught by all women: "The one thing that was good was that you never had to refrain from saying something in class for fear of seeming smart and therefore losing the love of the boys." As Gordon says, Catholic girls grew up in a separate but equal world, even if in liturgical terms they were always second-class citizens. In the Catholic Church the priest is the sacred personage, and only the male can be a priest. The nuns were less potent, less distant and magical. They were like members of an asexual harem.

So Catholic girls could not become the sacred personage. The best they could hope for was to become a nun . . . or a wife. Along the way, of course, they could always make stops at schoolteacher or nurse or secretary. Most of the girls I saw still resembled Donna Reed and her attractive clone, Shelly Fabares, and the majority of shows on television were westerns and comedies—*Gunsmoke* and *Rawhide, McHale's Navy* and *The Dick Van Dyke Show.* But people were beginning to see what the American dream might imply for women, and by August of 1963 these same girls watched images on television of hundreds of thousands marching on Washington, and they listened to Martin Luther King, Jr. speak words they had never heard on *Father Knows Best* or *Ozzie and Harriet.* They heard a new music and probably sensed that the times *were* changing, even if they weren't sure exactly how. The sixties began with Fats Domino, Elvis Presley, the Kingston Trio, and Fabian, but within a few years the Beach Boys, Martha and the Vandellas, and Marvin Gaye were sharing the public stage with Carole King and Peter, Paul, and Mary. All the girls had been required to read *The Good Earth* in the eighth grade, and some of them discovered that even Pearl S. Buck was disenchanted with the facts of life for American women. She described their plight as the "Carol Kennicott problem," alluding to the protagonist of Sinclair Lewis's novel *Main Street.* According to

Buck, modern American women had been stripped of their work and of their moral stature.

All of this brings me back to Ginger, but by no means am I suggesting that she dumped me out of some feminist rebellion or because of a growing awareness of the boundaries she was able to step beyond. I doubt that she had read Betty Friedan's *The Feminine Mystique* or had even heard of it. Maybe she was merely one of the girls that John Dos Passos describes as flocking out of a James Dean film "dizzy with wanting." Anything was possible, although I never saw a book in her hand and never heard her mention James Dean either.

Ultimately, I suppose I believe that the times may have made us all dizzy with wanting, and the Bronx merely intensified our intuition that there was something else we were born to do, some other place we were meant to be, and some other person we were destined to meet. So, Ginger dropped me for an older guy. At the time, the pain felt good, sharp and enlightening—although, of course, really it was none of those. I nurtured that pain for a while, not knowing I would meet up with her twice again before high school was finished, and the pain would take a new and duller, but much more illuminating, form.

In the year before I saw her again, I tried to get used to Lyndon Johnson in John F. Kennedy's place. I listened to the Beatles, read *Lord of the Flies* and *The Merchant of Venice,* and saw Mary Viangello and Paul Bowtons slipping along a back alley together.

Paul Bowtons was effeminate. The fact that he was a couple of years older than I or my friends didn't stop any of us from making fun of him. We called him "Blow tons," and when he tossed his head like a nervous colt, his auburn hair flicking back across his freckled forehead, we laughed and taunted him with more intensity. It was rumored that he once got fed up and actually fought someone, and even though none of us witnessed the fight, we didn't want to test him too far because he might break. Even the dullest and most sadistic among us realized that fighting Paul Bowtons would be a losing battle, not because he was tough—although for all any of us knew he could have been a tenacious fighter—but because fighting with him would have forever linked one of our names to his. There were simply too many rumors about what he had fondled and sucked on to make such a fight heroic. So we taunted him cruelly, viciously, but carefully, always making sure we were aware of some invisible line we should not cross. We didn't want to be touched by him.

Mary Viangello was a plain girl, but she had ample breasts. Of course, *ample* is a subjective term, and to the eighth-grade boys I knew, just about all breasts might have seemed ample, but Mary's, I suppose, were more than ample. She had a pleasant face, unremarkable and unassertive. She could have been an Italian peasant, and my guess was that she was not very far removed from some village in Sicily. Except for one story, she might have remained as unnoticed as Paul Bowtons was noticed. The story came from Johnny DeCaprio. We called him "Mizer"—he must have failed to lend money to someone of wit sometime during those grade school years—but the nickname, which may have called his generosity into question, didn't seem to make anyone doubt his word. Johnny's story was simple, and he told it often. One night he had walked the few blocks from Villa Avenue to Harris Field with Mary Viangello. They had stopped along the bridge that spanned the train yard and kissed. When they got to Harris Field, Johnny looked at her and said, "Let me see your tits." Perhaps to his surprise, she did. And she let him feel them there in the darkness with nothing but the wind whispering to them on that open field. Nothing much else happened between them, but what did happen was enough for Johnny's story and enough to create the image of Mary Viangello that we all then carried with us—her blouse open, her

breasts magnificently free in the night, the vast spaces of many
football fields surrounding her.

Paul Bowtons and Mary Viangello, then, had something in common: in our minds they were both tainted, but they were both legends. One we feared, and the other we longed for, even though, in a
sense, they both stood for the same thing to us. If we were looking
for simple definitions of masculine and feminine—and I think we
were—neither Paul nor Mary made things easy. He challenged our
sense of the prescribed sexual order of things, and she did too. We
feared him because he was different or perhaps because we feared
he wasn't. Mary, on the other hand, was all female, but she seemed
too obliging and therefore all too mysterious in her lack of mystery.

Every Saturday during the school year I delivered prescriptions
for a drugstore on Seventy-seventh Street and Lexington Avenue in
Manhattan, and on a cold, grey afternoon in which the wind swept
between the buildings, I saw them together. It was about four in the
afternoon, about two hours before I got off from work and rode the
IRT back up to the Bronx. The sky, which had been dark all day, was
turning sodden as well. My last delivery had been the strangest of
my six-month-long career. I had just delivered a package to a
woman on the sixteenth floor of a Park Avenue apartment building
and walked down the hall to wait for the elevator when a mainte-
nance man dressed in a beige uniform that made him look like a
hospital orderly opened the door from the stairwell and beckoned
to me. "Come here," he said in a heavy Spanish accent. "I want to
ask you something."

He looked down a few inches below my belt buckle and said,
"I'd like to suck on it." I was young, caught between the stairwell
and the hallway, with little natural wit for such situations. So I
looked at him, my mind racing for the right thing to say as I had visions of his taking out a switchblade when I refused his kind offer,
and all I could think of was, "Why would you want to do *that?*"

Even as I said it, I felt foolish. I'm not sure what I expected him to say. Would he give a long psychological or genetic explanation of his desires? He wasn't a philosopher, though, and merely said, "I like it." But the word *eet*, as he pronounced *it*, entered my consciousness at the same time as Mother David's admonition: "Never answer a question with a question!" That applied, I supposed, even to questions framed as statements. Finally, he seemed as stunned by my question as I had been in asking it, for he just nodded when I said that I had to get back to work and would probably see him again soon, as if we were parting amiably after an awkward date.

On my way back to the drugstore I caught a glimpse of Mary Viangello and Paul Bowtons skipping down the steps of a church on Lexington Avenue and running along Seventy-fifth Street. They appeared to be holding hands and laughing. She turned and whispered something into his ear. "C'mon," he seemed to say, tugging on her arm, and they were gone around a corner, as if I had imagined them. By the time I got back to work and entered the basement to arrange some stock, I felt as if I understood something that I had not before. I can't say even now what that something was, but I can say I had come closer to accepting my own confusion and the simple fact that there were certain things I might never understand—one of them being where desire led some of us.

Somehow I never felt it odd that Mary Viangello and Paul Bowtons didn't acknowledge each other in school or anywhere in the neighborhood, as far as I saw. I never told my friends that I had seen them together. I'm not sure why. It seemed like admitting that you had seen your sister naked—not something you were supposed to see, even in an accidental glimpse.

Most of the boys I grew up with in the Bronx were easy enough to read; their dreams and motives appeared fairly clear. They wanted to be strong enough to escape. They wanted to become old enough and wise enough to get on the road, any road out into the world. But girls were not as easy to understand. They often seemed to be happy where they were, calm and satisfied. They jumped rope, led cheers at games, skipped along, and laughed in tight circles, but often they appeared to be motionless, the still center around which we swirled.

Of course, I generally saw them from the outside, from a distance. Every now and again, though, because I had an older sister or because circumstances allowed me to eavesdrop in the lunchroom or near the park fence, I heard their stories in much the same way I heard those of my friends. Their dreams were shaped, I imagine, by the fictions they encountered on television, in the movies, in the apartment buildings around them. They invented new hairdos, French twists and beehives matched to pony tails. They rolled their hair in orange juice cans and sat in hot bathtubs with their new jeans on to make them shrink. They danced to *American Bandstand* each afternoon and did the Lindy and the Twist as they sighed over Jan and Dean. When they were young, they played school and fantasized about becoming nuns. On warm days after school they played Chinese jump rope and roller skated along the uneven sidewalks. They imagined themselves as the owners of candy stores. Like the boys, at times they too taunted the superintendents of the buildings, rang doorbells, or stole milk bottles and ran breathlessly and joyously down the streets as they were chased by shouts and threats. When they got older, they dreamt of ice skating at night in Central Park and sitting in the shadowy corners of fallout shelters. And of us, I thought. We daydreamed about scoring touchdowns in front of them, sinking free throws in the last seconds of a big game as they cheered, so I just assumed that girls could be explained by our definition of the world we found in the Bronx in the 1960s. It seemed logical to me that their mysteries were to be solved in relation to our dreams, that they all—Angela, Elka, Mary, Ginger, and the rest—waited for our next encounter.

The next time I saw Ginger was on November 9, 1965. I was stocking the shelves in Mr. Levi's grocery store on Valentine Avenue. It was a Tuesday, about half an hour before I was to get off from work, and I crouched in one of the aisles, stocking cans of Le Sueur peas on a grimy shelf, lazily stamping the price on top of each one as I listened to Barry McGuire sing in rasping and disgusted tones, "and you tell me over and over and over again, my friend, you don't believe we're on the eve of destruction." I believe that I prided myself then on understanding McGuire's cynicism very well and stamped each can an extra time or two in rhythm with the music. When the lights dimmed and then went out, and the music abruptly stopped, it seemed plausible that the end of the world had come, and with fitting irony Barry McGuire had announced it on a local FM station.

I went outside the store to see if anyone knew what was going on and saw something I had never seen before in the city—total darkness, not a light on in any apartment window or storefront, nothing to illuminate the deepening blackness until a car came up the side street and for an instant allowed me to see Ginger at the other end of the block, walking toward me and smiling. She mouthed the word "hello" and smiled again. The smile seemed to last in the fading light left by the car's headlights, but by the time she got close to me, I realized that she hadn't even seen me in the doorway of Mr. Levi's store. Her eyes were focused on a point over my left shoulder, and when I turned, I saw her new boyfriend.

I'm sure that if I had been a more sophisticated reader at the time, I probably would have seen myself as Joyce's young narrator in "Araby," but I had to rely on *Splendor in the Grass* for my images of lost love, and therefore it was Natalie Wood I saw disappearing into the incredible darkness. I was the hard-working Warren Beatty left behind. By the time I got home that evening, candles were already flickering in many windows, and an apocalyptic joy appeared to be spreading across the city. New Yorkers, it seemed, were taken out of their everyday torpor, awakened to a newer world, even darker than the one they imagined daily. Everyone expected the worst of New Yorkers, especially New Yorkers, so it was the residents of the city who were the most surprised, perhaps, by the goodwill, the patience, the generosity. More than one half million commuters were stranded on the stalled subway cars and elevators. People walked miles through the unlit streets to get home from work. The airports were shut down, Broadway shows were closed, newspapers canceled their morning editions.

But, as *Time* magazine later wrote, "The lost story of the longest night lay, indeed, in what didn't happen: there were no plane crashes, no train wrecks, no disastrous fires, no crime waves or looting sprees." When the blackout came to the city, it seemed to clear everyone's vision.

Except mine. That night in the double darkness I dreamt of Natalie Wood, standing on the Grand Concourse, waving her hand, a coy smile as she turned away from me and dissolved, blown like particles of my imagination into the past and the future. I stood transfixed, stuck on my block as the Independent Subway train rattled the grating beneath my feet and the world moved around me. I woke up the next morning disappointed that the sun was shining, that the television and radio worked, and that school and business would proceed as usual. I longed for another blackout in the Bronx—to be stunned by change, perhaps to see another mysterious smile in the unexpected darkness, and this time to be altered forever by it.

·····

Many of the faces seem the same, almond in the mixed light from the windows and the fluorescent bulbs. Shining hair reflects against lovely, enigmatic half smiles. They wear the same dark green plaid skirts and white blouses, their bodies arched as if they are waiting for the right moment to shed them for jeans and T-shirts. It is their eyes, though, great brown disks of anticipation and secret knowledge, that I remember so well.

These young girls, who will graduate in six months from St. Philip Neri, more than thirty years after I did, have different names than the girls I once knew—Srakhoo, Rodriguez, Reynoso, Martinez—but there are a few McLaughlins, Flanrahans, and Coluccis, too. Whatever their names, their eyes are wide with dreams of the future and a knowledge of the present. When they envision the future, they tell me, they see themselves as lawyers, doctors, archaeologists. One says she will be a brain surgeon, another a Supreme Court justice. Accountants, singers, teachers, pediatricians. Only one wants to be a secretary, and a few say that they will never marry or have children. Some imagine they will end up dreaming their golden dreams in California; some will return to the warmth of the Dominican Republic; some will always remain in the Bronx, they say, despite its drug dealers, stray bullets, unsafe shadows.

To most of them, their Bronx is much like mine was to me. It is the only home they know. It is familiar and therefore as safe as they can expect life to be. It is filled with their friends and all the comforting faces of teachers, family, shopkeepers, neighbors. For them, the Bronx is, at its worst, still "a place that teaches you how to live."

It is also a landscape that induces abstracted gazes, but these girls, three decades after the ones I knew, have different daydreams—to be doctors, lawyers, artists. Or perhaps, back then, I never had the chance to find out what the girls' dreams were. Maybe theirs were much like the boys', like these girls', varied and unpredictable and individual.

As the heavy doors to St. Philip's creak slowly to a close, I see a young woman standing in the frame. Her face could be my sister's at her graduation in 1960. The same blue eyes, looking down as if she is ready to raise them at any moment toward an unexpected guest. The same brown hair, a dark wave crashing to her shoulders. The same smile, the lips tugged together and curving upward toward laughter. Narrow-shouldered, slim as the slant of doorlight, ready to leave, she is the image of my sister in the Bronx then. With a few inches of light left, she looks up, her eyes clear and patient, and smiles at me as if she regrets my going, our mutual turning into memory.

CHAPTER 5

Mount St. Michael *and*
Other Unanswered Questions

I felt like I was sort of disappearing.
> —J. D. Salinger,
> *The Catcher in the Rye*

Make me thy lyre, even as the forest is.
> —Percy Bysshe Shelley,
> "Ode to the West Wind"

I started high school a few months before John F. Kennedy was murdered and a couple of days after Johnny Beaujolais threw a cherry bomb through the open kitchen window of Steve Marcelonis's apartment. Beaujolais was dark and fat and unashamedly malicious. He didn't seem to care if anyone liked him, and for that reason some people apparently did.

He was older than my friends, so we didn't know him except as a face—until he tossed the cherry bomb. Then, for a brief time, like Rip, he became famous. His fame didn't come from throwing the explosive, blood red and the size of a ping-pong ball, through a window where actual human beings were sitting down to eat supper—although most of us were impressed by such boldness—but rather from the fact that Mr. Marcelonis pursued him for what seemed like the entire fall. Every time he saw Johnny, the pursuit would begin again, always with the same call to battle, "Hey, you, bomb thrower!"

Of course, this story may seem apocryphal to those who would ask, "Why didn't Mr. Marcelonis just go to Beaujolais's house and tell his father, or why didn't he call the cops and let them handle it in their muddled way?" I don't have any answers to those questions. All I have is the story of Mr. Marcelonis's mad, illogical pursuit.

When I read *Catch-22* for the first time in my senior year of high school, I had a sense of deja vu. Nately's whore had the same pre-posterous tenacity that Mr. Marcelonis showed that fall three years earlier. Like Nately's whore, Mr. Marcelonis might appear at any moment: he might spring from a shadow-filled alleyway as if he had been waiting there for hours, perhaps all day, maybe off and on for days, and scream "Bomb thrower!" as he reached for a white scrap of neck that flew out of his reach like a fragment of paper blown by a gust of wind.

As far as I know, he never caught Johnny, but even though at first we identified with Johnny, finally it was Mr. Marcelonis who captured our imaginations, for he was our first taste of obsession. I remembered the night watchman who had chased Patty, Steve, and me, but Mr. Marcelonis raised the idea of the chase to another level. His obsidian eyes became as haunting as T. J. Eckleburg's in *The Great Gatsby.* With him, the chase grew into myth. It appeared as if he were around night and day, that his sole vocation was to hunt Johnny Beaujolais. The way I imagined it, that was all he dreamed of as he pounded dented Pontiacs with a rubber hammer in some body shop. He thought of it as he spoke to his wife at the dinner table, a glance at her and a glance at the half-open window. Perhaps Mr. Marcelonis showed us that adults could take us very seriously, or maybe he simply demonstrated a monklike devotion to a cause.

We may have wanted to have some reason for single-minded devotion. For me, though, he was Heathcliff and Ahab, impaled by the idea of revenge.

Mr. Marcelonis had an escarpment of dark hair around a pink skull that was about the size of a small cantaloupe and sat upon a thick neck attached to a squat frame. He looked like Friar Tuck in overalls. Physically, he was what Johnny Beaujolais would probably become by the time he was fifty years old. They were like son and father, audacity transformed into obsession.

I never saw Mr. Marcelonis or Beaujolais much after the fall of my freshman year, but stories of the renewed chase were told every few months as if the enmity between the two were really love, beautiful and enduring. I was taken by their story because of the wonderful absurdity it suggested. They were never important characters in my life, any more than Jimmy Bufano or Tommy Murray were, but their story had an enigmatic quality, and, for me, life was a collection of dark mysteries, myths, and stories—from the Holy Ghost and the Blessed Trinity to the secrets of sex and manhood. Most of us entered high school a bit dazed, our heads spinning with tales of grails and archangels.

The last time I saw Mr. Marcelonis and Johnny Beaujolais I was in my sophomore year of high school. Mr. Marcelonis's ridge of hair was bleached grey, and Johnny Beaujolais's pompadour was receding into a widow's peak, as if one year of hide-and-seek was enough to mark them both forever.

I had just gotten off the D train and was walking out of the underground into the dusty light. Under my arm was a copy of Samuel Eliot Morison's *Admiral of the Ocean Sea*, a biography of Columbus that I had on permanent loan from the Forty-second Street Public Library. I was running my fingers along its scratched blue cover as if it were a rocky coastline and I were a blind man reading its contours. I remember the smell of the book as I held it to my nose while I rode the train—the odor of wood pulp and dark secrets. Even with the little I had read of the book in the library and in the subway, I sensed that Morison's account of Columbus's life was a story of dream and obsession, a man consumed by his desire to discover. At that time, the Columbus story seemed to be about courage and escape. It wasn't until a few years later, when I read the book again, that I suspected there were other ways of seeing Columbus—as a man who let his dream turn him into a brute, who never really knew what he had found, who out of stubbornness let others discover what he had actually stumbled upon. Then, though, it seemed enough to admire his unyielding optimism. Later, it became necessary to create an even deeper faith, a belief that it might be possible to discover what you didn't know you were looking for. A luck born of seeing.

So there I stood in the afternoon light, which fell like a yellow stain on the buildings around me, the feel of the book in my hand, the memory of its marshy smell in my nostrils, when Johnny Beaujolais and Mr. Marcelonis came into view. I was on the corner of the Grand Concourse and 200th Street. Beaujolais was walking toward me down the Grand Concourse from the north. Mr. Marcelonis was walking up the hill from the east. It was like a scene in a Charlie Chaplin film, hunter and hunted innocently moving toward convergence, and I was there watching as if I were enjoying a Saturday afternoon matinee at the Ascot Theater.

I stepped back a few feet, recognizing that the timing would be perfect. They would reach the corner at exactly the same instant. Perhaps, if fate had a cinematic sense, the two would bump into one another, even get their arms and legs entangled, crash to the pavement, and when they were on the ground in a comic lovers' embrace, they would gaze into each other's eyes in a recognition like that of someone waking up in a stranger's arms.

Johnny reached the corner first, a second before Mr. Marcelonis did, and was looking south toward Fordham Road. Mr. Marcelonis struggled to the top of the hill, wheezing and looking down at his shoes. Beaujolais paused as if he heard his name called, hesitating in his step just enough for Mr. Marcelonis to bump into him. Then something happened that was better than anything I had imagined. They didn't knock each other to the ground. Mr. Marcelonis didn't scream "Bomb thrower!" and lace his pudgy fingers around Beaujolais's neck. Beaujolais didn't disappear in a puff of smoke.

They simply walked on. In a hiss of breath Mr. Marcelonis whispered, "Watch it," and Johnny Beaujolais, unhearing, continued to look south. Neither of them saw the other. I was the one who had done the seeing, the recognizing of possibilities. With my copy of *Admiral of the Ocean Sea* under my arm, I stood there happily, watching each of them in turn until they fell from the horizon like a part of the world that would return the next day and the next, repeating their story in a perfect dance of anticipation.

I entered Mount St. Michael in 1963, dreaming of Columbus, dreaming of Mr. Marcelonis and Johnny Beaujolais, hoping to find a specific reason to run or something particular to chase. I expected hazings by upperclassmen and tests of my courage, intelligence, and resourcefulness. I was prepared to have some senior try to sell me a pass to use the elevator (I knew there wasn't one) or to convince me that the dean of discipline would never find out if I skipped out of Spanish class one day (I didn't know until later that Brother Charley Patrick, the dean of discipline at the Mount, eventually found out everything, saw everything, knew even our most hidden thoughts, it seemed). So I entered high school wary and watchful, believing in the power of the unknown. Like Yossarian keeping an eye out for Nately's whore, I scanned the horizon for whatever would hunt me, be it Mr. Marcelonis or a cruel upperclassman.

Cruelty seemed an ordinary part of life. It was everywhere we looked. We found it in our fathers' eyes after they came home weighed down with work and drink. We heard it in our own conversations on the playgrounds. We saw it everyday in the class-rooms throughout elementary school. A few brothers and nuns were profoundly kind and loving, some were harmlessly inept, but a couple were truly demonic—and they were the ones who haunted our daily existence. Brother Boniface, our seventh grade French teacher, was such a man.

Boniface had slick dark hair and was tall, pale, and soft. He had a doughy complexion, rounded at all the edges but with none of the jollity often ascribed to chubby people. He spoke with a sneering lisp, an inflection that rose up like a sharpened dagger. In his class I learned little French, but I developed the art of watchfulness. Brother Boniface was a master of sarcasm, finding the most vulner-able spot and pricking it with the sharpest words. Each day, his class was submerged in fear.

"What does the word *illettré* mean, Mr. Slater?"

Silence.

"What's the problem, Mr. Slater, too much time jumping rope with the girls and not enough doing homework? Or could it be that you're just stupid?"

A more dangerous silence.

Blood exploded into Slater's face, fueled by both shame and anger. Of course, it was easier to accept being called stupid than un-masculine, but Boniface, with a pointed economy, had wounded him in both ways. We all sat there thinking, "Being called stupid isn't so bad, but here's Brother Boniface, the most effeminate of all our teachers, certainly more so than any of the nuns, challenging someone else's sexuality." We all sat there silently, though, hoping, "Don't look at me, stick with Slater. Torture him if you must until, mercifully, the bell rings. In the name of the Father, the Son, and the Holy Ghost, Amen."

On this day Boniface pranced in front of us, his eyebrows arched, and we were all wary. Except for Gerald "Gump" O'Mannly.

Gump had somehow let himself slip back into a state of antediluvian innocence in the last seat in the third row. He had for a moment forgotten the danger, and by the time the dam broke it was too late for him to repair the damage. Out of the corner of my eye I saw Gump smile, heard him giggle, and caught the white flash of an exchanged note. Gump realized his personal catastrophe a split second after I did. All of a sudden he seemed to be alone in midair, a cartoon character who sees the chasm only after he has run far off the edge of the cliff.

Brother Boniface stood over him.

"Mr. O'Mannly?" His voice purred like an oiled machine. "A love note, perhaps?" Forty-two faces twisted into sickly smiles. The class pulse sped up, mouths went dry, armpits moistened. Then there was that awful collective thrill, the smell of blood. Like all good Catholics we prayed fervently for the martyr, hoping the beast would be satisfied before he eyed us.

Boniface turned his back toward us and walked to the front of the room, his robes swishing against the desks, his crucifix bobbing at his side. He faced us and smiled. Acid ran through our intestines.

"Mr. O'Mannly, come up here please." He said it sweetly, as if it were possible that he planned to forget the whole matter and forgive the transgression. But the silence was as thick as a dust cloud, our breathing shallow in anticipation of what we knew would happen. Gump knew, too. As he shuffled up the aisle, he reminded me for an instant of Boniface, soft and white, but somehow I already saw Gump's curly brown hair and open Irish face framed in a gallery of martyrs.

"Bend over, Mr. O'Mannly." He said it in the kind of gently encouraging tone one might expect to hear an Oxford-educated Japanese interrogator use on a downed British pilot in an old war film.

O'Mannly bent over the front desk and looked briefly at the forty-one faces fastened on his shrinking smile. Brother Boniface went to the supply closet as slowly as someone performing a gesture in a beloved ceremony. Reaching into the shadows, he pulled out a wooden paddle, eighteen inches long, six inches wide, and two inches thick. It had the useful, polished look of an instrument carved out of oak.

Boniface planted himself behind Gump, a little to the side, spreading his feet wide, like a priest who has left the baptismal font behind to stand in as a cleanup batter for a sandlot team. He moved the fingers of his left hand along the paddle, caressing for a moment the perfect smoothness of the wood, and then his right hand shot out like a viper's fangs from the black folds of his clerical robes. He grabbed the paddle and raised it high, lifting it away from his body. Down it came, swiftly and with a loud *thwack,* a sound that seemed to crack the silence even before the wood ever touched Gump. We jerked back at the same instant, pulled by the same string of sympathy and fear. It happened again. And once again.

By the fourth time Brother Boniface raised his arm, tears had welled up in Gump's eyes. Along with everyone else, I looked intently into the grain of my desk as if the answer to some complex algebra problem lay hidden there. Each time Boniface raised his hand, he took longer to let it descend. This time he stopped.

"Mr. O'Mannly, get some paper towels from the bathroom and clean that up!"

As Gump left the room, the lunch bell rang, and we walked past the spreading puddle near the front desk on our way to the cafeteria in the basement.

By the time I reached Mount St. Michael High School years later, I was thus prepared for various forms of cruelty and humiliation, so I was surprised that not many of the upperclassmen seemed to have time to inflict pain. As a matter of fact, they didn't seem to notice my existence. And there were fewer Bonifaces, or they were easier to avoid most of the time.

About one thousand boys attended the Mount. A few were my friends from St. Philip Neri Elementary School, but most were strangers. I felt small in every respect, compared with the numbers of students, the size of the buildings, the breadth of the campus. For that matter, I was small—barely five feet tall and one hundred pounds only when I was weighed with all my clothes on. The suspicion that one day I would get to be about six feet tall didn't matter much when just about everyone in the school towered over me. I was a little kid with a blond crew cut, and most of my classmates, it seemed to me, had already burst into puberty with deep voices and the beginnings of beards.

It was Mr. Tricario, our social studies teacher, who guided me through that first year, like an older brother nudging me into the world. He was tall and spoke in a gravelly New York accent rough enough to let him get away with any kindness without ever appearing to be too soft or weak. He always seemed *about* to smile, a laugh lurking in every expression. He would rap me on the head with the gem side of his Iona College ring when I wasn't paying attention, or he would bring me into the lesson with a gentle piece of sarcasm. When I gave a foolish answer, he would tilt his head to the right, angle his eyes toward the ceiling, and tighten his lips in mock despair. But no raps on the head or bits of facetiousness could hide his gentle character or real enthusiasm for what he did. He had a genius for authority, commanding our attention and respect. His humor suggested to me an unlimited optimism about youth, about what we might do, despite our foolish gravity and grave foolishness. His manner taught me that I would have to take myself both more seriously and less so as the years went along.

Outside the friendly combativeness of Mr. Tricario's class, the campus itself seemed vast with its four big buildings. The central building—a four-story administration and classroom building made of brick and cement turrets connected by a walkway to the gymnasium—had a cluster of trees in front of it and an elegant set of white steps, bisected in the middle by a small garden area and a statue of St. Michael fighting Satan, that led up to the vaultlike front doors, which had the school seal and motto ("To the Stars through Achievement") embossed over them in Latin. I often gazed up at the statue as I entered school in the morning and wondered about my namesake. I looked up the definition of our name—"who is like God"—but I couldn't decide if this phrase was an ironic question to deflate pridefulness or a heroic description of those who carried the name.

There was also a dormitory, for in the 1960s students still boarded at both the grade school and the high school. During my four years at the Mount the dormitory building was nearly as much of a mystery as the residence hall for the brothers. All of these buildings were situated on a twenty-six-acre expanse of land that covered four city blocks. A few baseball fields, a football field, a track, a handball court, and other facilities were carved onto that land between Murdock and Nereid Avenues. On all sides were lines of telephone poles and two-family houses. All of it was technically still part of the Bronx, but not the one I knew.

The most threatening building for me in my first year at the Mount was the gymnasium. I loved sports and was good at them, but because I was on the verge of puberty, and most of the other boys seemed to me to be covered in hair, I felt like a boy among men in the locker room. I did my best to be inconspicuous in the shower and dressing rooms, but it didn't always seem possible to glide through those rooms as invisible as I would have liked to be. Gym class itself was often fun when I could forget the terrible unveiling that came at the end of it. I could usually do more pushups and situps than my classmates. I could climb the rope in the center of the gym more easily than many of the brawnier boys. I hated our gym teacher, though. I'm confident that just about everyone in the school did. He had the smile of a Marine drill instructor and the eyes of a prison guard. The only time he truly seemed to enjoy his work was when he lined us all up for calisthenics and marched between the lines giving us orders.

"I want to see everyone breaking a sweat here. I want you to bend all the way when I say touch your toes. I want your nose to touch the floor on pushups. I want . . . I want . . ."

He would scrape his hand through his short-cropped blond hair, stretching the tanned skin of his forehead. Then his voice would get a little lower, more threatening.

"Everyone is supposed to wear a jock strap, ladies. Anyone who forgets to wear his jock will have to run three laps."

As he said the word *ladies* with a hint of falsetto, he walked in back of the lines of boys. All we could hear was the squeal of his sneakers on the hardwood floor somewhere behind us. Silence. Then he would yank down someone's gym shorts, usually exposing the fact that the boy had forgotten to wear his jock or had left it at home, and had taken his chances with underwear or a bare ass. Red-faced and pulling his shorts up from around his knees, the boy who was caught would do his laps. The rest of us forced smiles to show we weren't worried, but we also weren't sure who would slip up next or what humiliation was in store for us.

By my sophomore year I had gone through puberty and looked very much like my peers, so gym became just another chore in a day of classes, as it was for most of the other boys. My day began at about 7:15 A.M. with a ride on a city bus that took me across Mosholu Parkway to 205th Street, where I picked up the number 16 to get to Mount St. Michael. I usually met Frankie Bartoletti on the Grand Concourse, and we walked together to Bedford Park Boulevard to wait for the bus. Frankie always carried his briefcase and wore a broad, gleaming smile. We all wore jackets and ties, but

Frankie's were carefully pressed. Without fail, his thick, dark hair was neatly combed, parted with a geometric precision. His books were stacked perfectly in his black attaché case with the polished brass locks. His homework, immaculate and always done on time, never had those crimped angles and erratic lines that mine had from being susceptible to the quick stops and bounces of the bus.

Frankie and I were good friends that year. I may have liked him because he reminded me of the order and discipline that a Catholic education seemed to mean then. It's not that I relished order and discipline, but like many of my friends I felt that I knew what the alternative to Catholic high school was in New York City. In the 1960s, eighth graders in Catholic elementary schools had to apply to Catholic high schools—a frightening process for most of those students.

We sent in our applications with our grades and achievement scores and waited. Most people applied to four or five schools, a first choice and a last. Then it was a matter of waiting for a thick envelope, one that required some effort to pull from the narrow apartment house mailbox. The thin envelopes meant rejection, which for some at St. Philip Neri and other elementary schools meant there was no alternative but public education. *Public school* had the same sound to our ears as *state prison*. At fourteen we believed that going to a public high school meant failure—not a simple failure either, but a terrible, irrevocable one. So we waited, our eyes on the slots in the mailbox, praying to be one of the chosen ones.

Those who I recall did not get accepted—Jimmy Keane, John Knecht, Tommy Slater, Jimmy Bufano, and others—we looked on with pity, as if they had announced to us that they had a disfiguring terminal disease. We didn't know what to say. Some students who did not make the grades but whose parents had a bit of money went to Bedford Park Academy, a small private school on the corner of 200th Street and the Grand Concourse. Once, it had been a house on a small hill overlooking the slope that led to Webster Avenue and the Botanical Gardens beyond it, but now it was a school for young men who had been discipline problems—their parents' last resort. When we walked home for lunch from St. Philip's, we would see the young men who went to the academy—their jackets thrown over their arms, their ties pushed inside their shirts, their hair slicked back—as they smoked cigarettes and flicked them from the overpass at the cars below.

I was accepted into all of the schools I applied to, but Mount St. Michael was my first choice. Brother Bruce, our principal at St. Philip's, convinced me not to apply to the Jesuit-run Fordham Prep that most of us considered the best high school in the area. I remember feeling a pang of regret that Brother Bruce assumed I was not a serious enough or gifted enough student to spend the next four years at that prep school housed in a beautiful stone building right in the midst of Fordham University's Rose Hill campus. But I quickly forgot my regret when I pulled the other thick envelopes from my mailbox. It wasn't until four years later, when I was a student at Fordham University, that I wondered again what it would have been like to spend my four years there with Al Arater, the smartest boy to graduate from my elementary school class.

So Mount St. Michael was a compromise, I suppose, like choosing to be a graphic designer rather than an artist, or an electrician rather than an engineer, the choice forced on my father by circumstances. Maybe it was just a realistic redesigning of my definition of self. Or perhaps it suggested that I had not defined myself sharply enough at that point. Whatever the case, each weekday morning, except for religious holidays, I ended up flashing my bus pass at an indifferent city driver as Frankie Bartoletti flashed his smile behind me.

·····

The central part of my life when I started high school was sports. I loved football and basketball. I dreamed each night of running, of scoring baskets and catching passes. The rumbling of the D train outside my window became the distant roar of that future crowd in Madison Square Garden. But with this dream, too, I had to compromise. Fairly soon after my freshman year, I had to accept the fact that I would not be a professional football or basketball player: I was too small make either of the teams. By my sophomore year I had grown about six more inches, and I made it up to the last cut of the JV basketball team; out of the fifteen left on the day of final cuts, twelve made it. By my junior year I was resigned to playing Catholic Youth Organization basketball, and I had also begun to work at a variety of jobs during the summer and the school year.

Different dreams began to fill my life. I still loved sports and played basketball every chance I got at P.S. 8, near Mosholu Parkway, but other things captured my attention as well. Girls, at the back of my mind for a few years already, began to fill my daydreams. Often during my freshman and sophomore years I found myself lost in thought as the bus pulled up to Mount St. Michael, and I had to quickly put my book bag in front of my pants to hide an erection that I was certain everyone in the vicinity would notice.

Although girls were never too far from my thoughts, books started to capture my attention, too. In Brother Eugene's freshman English class, we studied *The Merchant of Venice*. When I opened the play and read, "In sooth, I know not why I am so sad," I knew I was in a familiar world, but one that was different, too. I found the "sooths" and "want-wits" a bit confusing, but I felt a kinship with Antonio because of his sadness. I understood his dull ache: "What stuff't is made of, Whereof it is born / I am to learn." Shakespeare gave me a world both recognizable and totally foreign, and Brother Eugene seemed an undeniable part of that world. He was small and narrow shouldered; his eyes were like the unlit points of match sticks, and his mouth seemed permanently stitched into a half grin. As he swept back and forth in front of the classroom, leaving gusts of wind and words in his wake, his light brown pompadour stayed lacquered in place like a piece of polished marble. He would put his crucifix—hanging beneath the bone-white rectangle of Roman collar that scratched his neck—into a fold in his cassock, and his arms would fly up and his eyes ignite with enthusiasm. The words would burst from him:

> I hold the world but as the world, Gratiano,—
> A stage where every man must play a part;
> And mine a sad one.

It was impossible for Brother Eugene to look sad, though, for he looked like Dennis the Menace half grown, but with the same devilish expression in his face. After a few days reading the play, I forgot Brother Eugene's comic face and began to see and hear only the words. He made us memorize Portia's famous speech to Shylock in act 4:

> The quality of mercy is not strain'd
> It droppeth as the gentle rain from heaven
> Upon the place beneath. It is twice bless'd:
> It blesseth him that gives and him that takes.
> 'Tis mightiest in the mightiest: it becomes
> The throned monarch better than his crown.

As I listened to the words spoken in class and began to hear them in my own head—echoing against my father's silences when I read them at home on the living room couch—I felt just as I had in the first grade at St. Philip Neri's. We were all given a box of letters, each rectangular box containing hundreds of smooth little cardboard squares about the size of Scrabble pieces. I'm not certain now what the teachers expected us to do with them—learn the alphabet or make words, I guess—but what I remember most clearly is seeing the letters fly around the desks when Mother Concepta left the room on some errand. The letters flew, skimming like flat stones on a lake, falling like snowflakes in February, a storm of Zs and Ls floating everywhere. They splintered the air. They soared, banged into one another, crashed into the windows and blackboards, and drifted down into poetry and nonsense on the classroom floor. At the end of the year I had only three letters left—an S, a B, and a Q—but I learned to love the sight of those letters, the sound they made as they spun through the stale schoolroom atmosphere.

I began to write my own poems and stories, on scraps of paper during algebra class or in the back of my history notebook. At home, my father would tell me to do something, but I would be lost in thought until he would say, "Wake up. What are you always dreaming about?"

Usually in the gym or on the athletic field I fell into a mindless concentration on what I was doing, but even there sometimes I dreamed of stories. One evening at P.S. 8 I was thinking of a story I might write about an undersized basketball player whose talent went unrecognized by those around him when I slammed into the wall and broke my finger. When I went home, my mother was out, and I knew that I could not tell my father what had happened, so I kept my left hand in the pocket of my navy pea coat, one finger twisted away from the painful fist I had formed. In the living room, I whispered to my sister, Ginny, who understood immediately why I did not want to tell my father, for we both knew he would yell at me for being careless or, worse, would blame my mother for not being home. My sister took me to the doctor, who set my finger and put it in a splint. My father never found out that I had broken it, and when he asked, about a week later, what was wrong with my finger, I told him that I had twisted it playing stickball.

I continued to write my own stories, but I kept my eyes wide open, watching carefully for where the world might collide with my imagination. I was always on the lookout for narratives that matched my own confusion, that seemed to say it was a natural feeling. School provided so many answers to so many questions—why did God make me? what is a predicate nominative? what is the square root of 81?—that I longed not for answers, but for a moment of recognition, for stories in which I'd see my own face, my own life.

Brother Eugene made us memorize Shakespeare's words and recite them in front of the class, so we heard the words over and over as we stumbled through them and over them. A sad-eyed Vincent Tosti pulled at the bottom of his checkered sports coat as he repeated "his sceptre shows" over and over like a stuck record until he finally collapsed back into his seat. Robert DeGregorio didn't get past the first lines, and Claude Pennacchia didn't even try at all. But Pio Asterita surprised everyone by saying the words as if they were his own and he really meant them. For me, and maybe for some of the others as well, memorizing the words made them mine forever, words as beautiful and gentle as the rain they described. Words seemed to pour from the sky unexpectedly in the next few years.

In my sophomore year we read *Lord of the Flies.* The teacher made it into something like an algebraic problem, focusing on which boy symbolized what idea and what all the symbols finally added up to. Although I disliked math, I loved the book, partly perhaps for the solvable puzzle the teacher made of it, but mostly for the great, turbulent mystery *it* made of adolescence. The violence in the story seemed to reflect something in my own life, some ripping of seams. The novel seemed to acknowledge a cruelty and darkness, a chaos and terrifying wonder that went beyond the rules made for us.

In my junior year I fell headlong into the poetry of Percy Bysshe Shelley. I was swept away not so much by his writing, though, as by his life, or at least by my English teacher's description of his life. I've forgotten that teacher's name, but I can picture him readily as he stood before the class. The fact that he was a layman was unusual enough at Mount St. Michael, but the fact that he was young and strangely handsome made him truly different. He was as long necked and angular as Ichabod Crane, but he had a superb confidence that made his features seem untamed and appealing, as well as a smile that reminded me of my father's in those photographs of him when he was on Tarawa and Okinawa. His shock of dark hair fell into his eyes as he talked of the romantic poets. It seems now as if he spent the whole year on Shelley, Wordsworth, Keats, and Byron, but we must have covered all of English literature in that course. While the class surveyed British literature, I focused on Shelley, reading the biographies more avidly than the poetry. During that year I began to see Mount St. Michael as my Eton, and I thought about distributing my own pamphlets denouncing educational punishments and institutionalized religion. Even when the image of Charley Patrick forced me to reflect on the consequences of any form of rebellion, my daydreams led me toward a sympathy and admiration for Shelley and a desire to discover the same sort of existential faith, the skeptical idealism, that he seemed to find before he drowned in the Gulf of Spezia. When Shelley spoke in "The Revolt of Islam," I felt that he mouthed my thoughts:

> So without shame, I spoke: "I will be wise,
> And just, and free, and mild, if in me lies"

After three years of silence in the halls, of shined shoes, and of stark haircuts, I was ready, like Shelley, if I had it in me, to be a heretic, a nonconformist, to denounce the petty tyranny of my schoolmasters, to fall in love, to write, to run away.

J. D. Salinger, and mainly *The Catcher in the Rye*, held my attention in the beginning of my senior year. It wasn't an English teacher but my friend Jerome Mahon who gave me a copy of *Catcher*. When I began to read the novel, I saw Jerome in it. He had fashioned himself on Holden, and I realized, happily, that I was not the only person to use literary characters in such a manner. However, whatever rebellion Holden confirmed in me, made possible for me to imagine, I began my subversion slowly and modestly. My hair got a little longer, my language a bit more raw, my cynicism a shade sharper. Jerome, though, seemed to change overnight. He stared at everyone with the same mocking expression; he drank beer out of the side of his mouth as if he wanted the other side free to smirk; he was smart, but he did only the work he wanted to do. We all talked about what a waste of time certain subjects were, but he actually stopped studying whatever seemed stupid to him. During the next few years he drifted in and out of college, in and out of drugs, his character a shifting mixture of James Dean, Camus's Meursault, and Salinger's Holden Caulfield.

Jerome was a year older than I was, so he had finished All Hallows High School and was attending Hunter College when I was in my last year at Mount St. Michael. Both of us had been in high school the year before, but now it seemed to me that we inhabited two very different worlds. He didn't go to mass and confession, and he made it clear that he thought it all a lot of Dark Ages superstition. When he didn't have classes and his mother was at work, he lay on his couch listening to Jefferson Airplane on his headphones and smoking a joint until it was a burning eye that winked between his thumb and index finger. It wouldn't be unusual for him to answer his apartment door naked and red-eyed in the middle of the afternoon. He started playing the guitar and at times performed with Rip, who plucked the bass and sang with the same scratchy resonance that Mick Jagger did. When Jerome wasn't playing music, he always had the same look of weary expectation in his eyes, as if he knew someone would say or do something stupid before long. Like the rest of us, he wanted to leave the Bronx, but at a certain point he fell in love with what the Bronx offered him: a target for his sarcasm. There were just so many things the matter with the place. He spent much of his time, joint in hand, talking about getting out of the Bronx, but he clearly enjoyed the dull-witted people and ugly terrain for the specific focus they gave him. Without the Bronx, he may have had to look more carefully at himself.

Jerome ended up, years later, in San Francisco, sliding from one job to another until he settled on being a conductor on the cable cars, a job that suited him perfectly. He constantly moved but never went beyond the familiar. He seemed to like the fact that change and repetition were the same thing on the Powell and Mason line, that he was in motion but had accustomed targets to judge. Jerome survived the sixties and his own imagination in his way. Stories and my imagination helped me to survive both in high school and against the ever-encroaching outside world.

Brother Charles Patrick McNiff demanded subtle survival skills. Charley Patrick, as we all called him when he was definitely out of earshot, was the dean of discipline at Mount St. Michael during my last two years there. He had dark blond hair and the soft, round face of a murderer who had gotten religion. I was in my junior year when I first really became aware of him. I was reading part of *Moby Dick* for English, and I remember having to look up the word *ubiquitous*, which Melville uses to describe the white whale. It wasn't long before I noticed that Charley Patrick appeared to be ubiquitous. Students sighted him in different places at the same time during a given day. Everywhere I went, I saw him. He was outside the lunchroom as we walked in to eat. He was in the halls when we changed classes. He watched us as we got off the buses in the morning and as we left the school grounds in the afternoon.

In particular, though, I remember his bulky shadow in front of the doors to the cafeteria each day at lunchtime. He stood there, solid as a whale, round faced and hawk nosed, as we lined up and passed before him in single file. He inspected our shoes and hair, squinting to see if we had shaved closely enough and to judge how much space the barber had left between our collars and the backs of our hair. We had twenty-six minutes between classes to eat lunch. About five minutes were taken up with the inspection line, which left each of us about twenty minutes to get our food, eat it, and spend some time hanging out in the quadrangle outside the cafeteria. For much of the second half of my junior year and a good portion of my senior year I had even less time to eat my lunch because I never entered the inspection line leading to the cafeteria. It was the late sixties, and I was tired of getting my hair cut to specifications and tired of being inspected. So to avoid any encounter with Charley Patrick, I went to lunch late everyday. I would wait on the second floor by the window overlooking the cafeteria and watch for Charley Patrick to head back toward his office. After all the spying he had done on me, I felt that it was appropriate for me to observe him from a distance.

It was months, probably sometime into my senior year, before Charley Patrick found me out. He never actually caught me looking at him from the second floor, and he didn't see me walking in late to lunch. I was given detention by my Spanish teacher for failing to do my homework. Charley Patrick oversaw all detentions in the biology lab, where we were required to stand behind the long lab tables. We were not allowed to talk, read, or sit down. We stood for an hour and a half, not talking if Charley Patrick were in the room or talking out of the sides of our mouths if he had left on some errand. Most of us never sat down or turned around to talk, though, because he often left the room just to go outside the building and observe us from the windows that stretched along the back of the lab. My rebellion in that classroom on many a long afternoon was to read—to hold a paperback beneath the lip of the lab table and read while my eyes occasionally lifted to look out for Charley Patrick.

My hour and a half of detention for not doing my Spanish homework went by uneventfully. I positioned myself in the middle of the class, in the fourth row. My hair was a bit longer than anyone else's in the room, and I tried to be invisible, not even willing to dare fate by reading my tattered copy of *Cat's Cradle*. Charley Patrick never once looked in my direction. At 4:30 he sat at the teacher's desk in the front of the room and dismissed us row by row. He kept his eyes on some paperwork that he had in front of him as we marched out in silent, ragged lines. I felt a sense of exhilaration as I reached the door jamb, one second from the hallway, a few steps to the outer doors, then a short walk to the bus stop. But Charley Patrick caught me in midair, my foot between the lab room and the hallway.

"Mr. Pearson," he said, without ever looking up from his papers, "you need a haircut. That will be three days' detention. Be in my office tomorrow morning by 7:30 with a proper one."

I was surprised that he knew my name so readily, that he didn't have to resort to "hey you." The whole afternoon he had never once, as far as I knew, looked in my direction. Perhaps he had seen me days before, or even months, and he had been waiting from the time of his perception of that first follicle growth for this very moment, this perfectly timed moment, when he could catch me off guard. I had to dash for the bus to get home in time before the barber shop closed, and then I had to leave twenty minutes early for school the next morning. For the rest of the year I ate lunch on time, a little ashamed when I thought of Jerome Mahon, James Dean, Meursault, Holden Caulfield, and Shelley, but I told myself that I was biding my time, that I was imagining myself into rebellion, imagining a new self through books, seeing myself outside the classroom and in the larger world, trying to understand the relationship between the stories that swept me forward and the world I was entering.

Around the time I turned fifteen, the larger world meant work. I helped out occasionally at Drewsen's Delicatessen, delivering groceries to apartments in the area. Drewsen's had a big green delivery bike with an oversized basket welded onto the front. The basket was big enough to carry a box that contained three or four bags of food. I loved filling in for my friend Chris Young. Riding that bike under the overpass toward the apartment houses on Briggs and Valentine Avenues, rattling over the uneven roadway, was an exciting adventure in balance and speed. When I passed my friends, I waved like a man in a hurry, someone with important things to do. Hardly ever did I feel a pang of jealousy about the idle pursuits in which they were engaged.

My first real job was in Mr. Levi's grocery store. My friend Frank Fitzpatrick, who worked there, got me the job. It wasn't an auspicious beginning to my working career. I worked for a few hours stocking shelves, and then Mr. Levi sent me down to the basement to get some bottles of soda. I reached into a case of Cott Cream Soda and lifted one out by its neck. I heard the explosion and saw the index finger on my left hand at the same time. It appeared to be someone else's hand, the blood covering it, the bone jutting from the finger in a way that made me turn my glance away.

When I came up the stairs, my right hand tightly squeezing my left wrist, holding it upright like some strange red bouquet that everyone retreated from in horror, Mr. Levi didn't seem to know what to do. Weeks later, I found out that his main concern had been the fact that I did not have working papers. He slid his stubby fingers across his bald head and then wiped his hands on the greasy apron that did little to veil his protruding stomach. He called out in his high-pitched British accent to his wife, who stood at the cash register gazing dreamily at the headcheese, but she didn't offer any advice. Frank Fitzpatrick finally said, "I'll take him to the hospital, Mr. Levi."

And Frank did—in the basket of the Levis' delivery bike. Frank was always ready for an adventure, and the ride to the hospital, over potholes and around double-parked cars, was a roller coaster. The basket could hold a couple of grocery bags filled with bread and soda, and was therefore just large enough for me to sit uncomfortably with my legs dangling over the side, the metal edge cutting into the underside of my knees, as Frank bounced along toward the emergency entrance of Montefiore Hospital on 210th Street. By the time we arrived at the emergency entrance, the towel Mr. Levi had given me for my hand had turned a deep red. For some reason, the doctors never fixed the bone properly. They stitched up the finger, but the bone jutted out from that day forward, and the finger never regained its flexibility. At the time, though, I enjoyed the attention the bandage and sling gained me from Mr. Tricario in social studies class, from Ginger at the park, and even my friends as we waited for the school bus.

I went back to work for Mr. Levi after a couple of weeks and stayed at the store for about a year, until the Workman's Compensation Bureau contacted my mother about benefits. I was fourteen and did not have working papers, which made Mr. Levi liable for double indemnity. That meant he owed us $465, which he paid at $15 a month for the next three years or so. I moved on to other part-time jobs.

Frank told me about the job delivering prescriptions for the pharmacy on Seventy-seventh Street and Lexington Avenue. It was there that I did most of my dreaming of Columbus. On long deliveries that took me to lower Manhattan, I would hop a train all the way down to Battery Park and use my lunch hour to watch the ships sail out of the harbor. I would imagine myself on whatever vessels floated out from the middle of the widening Hudson into the Atlantic Ocean—merchant or cruise ships. I would see myself standing along the railing of a cruise ship that had just been directed by the boats away from the Twelfth Avenue piers, turning my gaze north to watch the George Washington Bridge grow smaller, then east to follow the peak of the Empire State Building above the other skyscrapers, past the New Yorker, the Victorian houses above the Palisades, Ellis Island, the Statue of Liberty. As I left the harbor, I would have the same feeling that my ancestors from Ireland and Germany probably had as they entered it and saw the golden flame of liberty lit against the fading sun—a sense of finding a new world and leaving an old one behind. The wind would sweep into my lungs as the statue faded to a spark in the distance, and New York City would disappear.

The drugstore job was only on Saturdays and didn't give me enough money, so eventually I had to quit, but I left reluctantly because it ended my excursions to the harbor. I took a job schooldays from three until six and all day on Saturdays at Martin's Butcher Shop, right next to Drewsen's Deli. For Martin's, I rode the delivery bike beyond the local apartment buildings. Two or three times a week I had to deliver fifteen- or twenty-pound roast beefs to delis around the Bronx so that they could cook them and slice them up for sandwiches. Those trips from 200th Street to Fordham Road and farther were like excursions into different worlds. I saw no familiar faces. The buildings were brick, but they were different buildings than I had seen before. Those rides were long enough for me to imagine myself as Youngblood Hawke or Huck Finn, heading out into the world, riding through one neighborhood and then another and another. Some nights I would dream of Columbus or of empty, rolling seas. My delivery route turned from road to river to night-skied ocean. One night, after working late, I dreamt I lounged on a beautiful cruise ship, polished and sparkling in the sunlight, next to Arthur Miller. He was reading a novel by E. L. Doctorow and half-heartedly listening to the conversation of his dowdy red-haired wife, a woman who catered to their two fat daughters, who roamed the decks. I woke up wishing I had dreamt that Marilyn Monroe was the woman sitting next to Miller in a bathing suit. And then I realized that I had to finish reading *The Crucible* for school the next day.

About half of my work hours I spent dreaming of adventure and the other half dreaming of girls. That left little time, of course, to concentrate on work, but luckily for me the tasks were routine and left my mind free to roam. I would think about myself with Frankie Bartoletti at a Mount St. Michael freshman dance on a Friday night, walking confidently up to a beautiful young girl and leading her out onto the floor. Bouncing along the cracked sidewalks as I rode the delivery bike, I was only rarely jolted from my daydreams, in which those girls saw me as the man I would become, an image that lurked, like my guardian angel, just over my shoulder.

The real dances were quite different, of course. Most of us would stand around self-consciously, trying to look indifferent to the girls who stood across the dance floor from us. We would huddle together like judges at a beauty pageant: this one was too fat, that one had cross-eyes, piano legs, a big nose, a flat chest. We waited for a slow song and then, with an affected casualness, walked over to a girl and asked her to dance. Often, at such dances Frankie and I would circle the floor and appraise the crowd. Sometimes we would circle the crowd the better part of the night, not even for a moment truly convincing ourselves that we were anything but scared to be rejected. Never in my freshman year did any girl seem to notice the real me that was about to emerge. They seemed to see only the kid with the crewcut who appeared to be younger than the other boys around him. By my sophomore year I dated occasionally, getting a girl's telephone number at a dance and then waiting two or three days to call. The only phone in our apartment was in the hallway adjacent to the living room. The thought of stumbling through a conversation with a girl as my family listened in was too much for me to bear, so usually I went to a pay phone around the corner or stretched the phone line into the bathroom and closed the door.

These telephone calls were rife with thrilling fears. I was afraid that the girl would not even remember who I was or, worse, that she would remember vividly, regretting many times in the past week ever having given me her number in the first place. I worried that there would be nothing to say, that even if she wanted to go out on Saturday night, we would have nothing to say to one another after the initial hellos. My palms would begin to sweat as my mind raced through a series of questions that seemed destined to elicit no response. And then I called. Invariably, the girl chattered on as if I were not even there, as if all it took to spark a blaze of conversation was one dry twig from me.

Until my senior year, when I bought a car, I'd have to take a city bus when I went on a date. Riding the bus meant long trips through strange neighborhoods, a movie, a sore arm from being unable to remove it decorously from the girl's shoulder once I had maneuvered so carefully to get it there, and a slice of pizza afterward. Then, of course, there was the good night kiss, which required as much sense of timing as the phone call, holding hands, or the request for a second date.

Finally, all the trauma seemed worth it, though, because of all the mysteries I encountered, girls were the most exciting. By my senior year I had a 1966 Pontiac Tempest, which I assumed would change my love life. It didn't change things much, although I did go out with a few different girls, falling into feverish crushes because of the way they smiled or canted their hips, the way they looked up at me or rubbed my arm when we sat in a restaurant. In my senior year I fell in love with the cherubic-faced T. C., partly for her sweet disposition but mainly because we had spent an hour walking together in a May rainstorm. I fell in love with the way the raindrops beaded on her upper lip and ran down the curve of her white throat. I fell in love with the sheer exuberance of standing in the rain with someone and getting drenched to the skin, letting the water go as deep as it desired.

Around this time I saw Ginger again. I was old enough to know that she didn't even remotely resemble Natalie Wood, but all those emotions I had felt at fourteen welled up again, and we started to date. She invited me to her prom, and in return I invited her to mine. Within forty-eight hours I knew that I had made a mistake, and perhaps she realized the same thing. I wasn't attracted to her or very much interested in her anymore, but the dresses and tuxedos got rented, the limousine paid for, and the reservations made at the Copacabana. We went to her prom, had a miserable time, and I lay in bed that night hoping to get the flu so that I would be unable to go to mine. At my prom we walked woodenly through our roles; we tried desperately to imitate real passion in the back seat of the limo, and when that was a clear failure, we opted to get drunk. One of us did, but I can't remember who now. Drinking, by that time in my life, had become a ritualistic part of most entertainments, certainly any dances. At the time, I saw drinking cheap wine with my friends before a Knights of Columbus dance as dangerous and liberating. I didn't think much about any connection to my father's unromantic drinking. The drinking I did with my friends was different, I told myself. We would never turn into our fathers. Even when we sat in Darby O'Gill's on a Friday night alongside some men who resembled our fathers, we assumed a much different future awaited us.

As for Ginger and me on that prom night, both of us, I'm certain, knew that some piece of our childhood was being left behind, and I was happy to discard it but at the same time sorry to see it disappear—perhaps because, although I did not see myself sitting vacant eyed in front of a boilermaker in a bar, I wasn't sure what picture I did see.

In my last two years of high school I realized that something was disappearing. I wasn't certain what was being lost, but I sensed that the war in Vietnam had something to do with it. As I moved toward senior year, the war seemed to get bigger and closer each day. In the spring of my sophomore year, twenty-five thousand students and others, some of them not much older than I was, marched in Washington to protest the killing. About twenty-five thousand American troops were in Vietnam then, but by my senior year there were more than four hundred fifty thousand, and fifteen thousand American soldiers had been killed, most of them in 1967. The war was fast approaching my doorstep, and many of my friends knew someone who had been killed or someone who was soon to embark on that thirteen-thousand-mile journey. The war was halfway around the world, but when the announcement came over the intercom in my senior year that Mike Cunyon—Mary's older brother, an admired athlete who graduated from the Mount a few years before I did—had been killed in Vietnam, it seemed very real. As a freshman I had watched him on the football field and seen him walk down the halls, godlike and seemingly untouchable. If they could get Mike Cunyon, how could the rest of us survive?

My last two years of high school were not filled with talk of the war, but it was always there, spreading into everything we did. We played sports, went to dances, drank beer along Mosholu Parkway, and dreamed our lives forward, but each night on the television news the story of Vietnam took up more and more time. Each day the papers told of a new battle or an aborted cease-fire. The narrative of the war kept drawing me in. Frank Fitzpatrick and others went into the service. After a fight with his girlfriend, a few beers, and hours of listening to the Shirelles sing "Soldier Boy," Frank joined the Marines. I was still in high school. In grade school, for a short period of time, we had been good friends. He was older than I was and treated me like a younger brother, always teasing me but watching out for me as well. Within a year he was home, out of the service. All I knew was that he had fought at Khe Sanh at the outset of the Tet Offensive and that his face appeared to be a mask, as if some creature had gotten inside of him and now peered out through eyes burnt colorless by a type of understanding that I didn't have.

I could imagine what he knew of casualties, body counts, and important battles. We all could. And so the war was always there. As we approached senior year, we took a step closer to Vietnam, not a war many of us could understand as our fathers had understood World War II. In a sense, it drew many of us together, and, as our fathers had with their war, we were able to find a common enemy: the wrongness of the Vietnam conflict. We began to relish simple phrases such as "military industrial complex," which allowed us to pinpoint a bogeyman.

In ways, the Bronx was safe. It was the known world. Vietnam suggested all that was dangerous and destructive outside our boundaries. To venture outside, it seemed to many of us, could be disastrous. Early on in high school, we were offered a good example of what could happen. Billy Slattery was pleasant looking, tall, smart, athletic. He played on the basketball and football teams. Many of us envied him until the summer after his sophomore year. On a trip across country with his family, he broke his back in an automobile accident. For months afterward, we saw him in the hospital, then in a wheelchair, and, finally, hobbling on crutches like a polio victim. He was a victim of the world, as indifferent as any war to grace and speed and strength. We looked at him, and our desire to leave childhood behind was chastened by an anticipation of what the future held.

As the war in Vietnam moved toward its inevitable escalation, the senior class went on a two-day retreat to a wooded enclave in the country. I recall sitting in the front bench of the chapel, listening to a middle-aged priest speak about the meaning of the word *retreat.*

"This is a time for each of you," he said, moving his gaze from one upturned face to another, "to step back from all your physical desires for a short while, to forget about worldly achievements. Put aside, for a moment, your plans, your dreams of success after college, thoughts of money or power or earthly love. Put your mind and heart on God's love. Think about divine love. Think about your mortality. That from dust you came and to dust you shall return. Think, young men, about death."

For the next two days we reflected upon last things. We discussed death and heaven. And hell, the darkness of sin. The failings of the flesh. That flesh decayed and the soul endured.

Each of us had his own small room, with a narrow bed and a set of drawers, a modern monk's quarters. We were given hours alone, and I spent mine lying on my cot near a window that overlooked a hillside, the sun warming one side of my face as I stared out at my future. The priest had struck the right words, I thought, *flesh* and *death.* I lay there thinking of girls and war.

It dawned on me then that most of my friends had become political and sexual in near identical leaps. Sometimes the two appeared to be one and the same, a revolution against parents, priests, brick buildings with or without official seals—against the idea of the Bronx itself. But on the last afternoon of the retreat I found myself saying, "Forgive me, Father, for I have sinned. . . . I am heartily sorry and will amend my life," and believing it, too.

.....

A short time after I returned from the retreat, I met Alma on my way home from Fordham Road with Frankie Bartoletti. I had gotten off early from my job as a waiter at Kohlman Hall, a residence for Jesuit brothers and priests on Fordham University campus. As I waited and washed dishes for dinner and sometimes for lunch, I used to watch in surprise as these religious men drank glass after glass of wine and beer and whisky. It was one more hint to me that the world was not what I had assumed it to be.

I had deposited some money in my account at the Dollar Savings Bank, and as we walked north in the direction of Poe Park, a thin young woman with freckles and auburn hair swung in front of me.

"Got a match?" she asked, holding a cigarette against her hair as if she were really asking something else entirely.

"I've got one at home," I said instinctively, even before I checked to see what time it was and if my father had gotten home from work already.

"Let's go," she said, and off we walked down the Grand Concourse, with Frankie and Alma's friend behind us. Those six blocks seemed to take longer than usual to walk. The small talk we made was all veiled with sexual implication; behind each word was hell and the darkness of sin. There was some hesitation in my mind, but certainly no retreat. When we got back to the apartment, Frankie and Alma's friend waited outside on the front stoop while Alma and I went in for the matches. Before we knew it, we found ourselves in the bedroom, sitting on my bed as she looked at my copy of Ian Fleming's *You Only Live Twice*, opened to the first page: "The Geisha called 'Trembling Leaf,' on her knees beside James Bond."

The next thing I knew, Alma's pants were off. I knew how James Bond's adventures affected me, but I was surprised to see how they affected her. I was amazed that *words* could transform the world in such a manner. I kissed her, fumbled with her sweatshirt, and stroked the mysterious tuft of hair that hid what was between her legs. I wasn't sure exactly what I was supposed to do, and although Alma seemed to know much more than I did about such things, she didn't tell me. Maybe from my casual act she assumed that I had experience. Maybe she was as innocent as I and just a girl for whom words meant a lot. I was getting a bit desperate. I believe I even began to think about skimming the first chapter of *You Only Live Twice* in the hope of finding some direction when the doorbell rang. Frankie hissed from the hallway, "I see your father across the street!"

Alma and her friend were gone before my father reached the door. Frankie and I sat there and said "hi" as he trudged up the steps. I saw Alma again a few times. She was from a small town in Alabama, but the city seemed to suit her. For some reason, though, I was never able to recapture that moment with her. It might have been that she sensed all I was really interested in as far as she was concerned was sex, or it might have been that I just never again had the opportunity to see her when I had a copy of an Ian Fleming novel with me.

Other girls drifted into my life as Alma drifted out of it. I fell in and out of love quickly. There was a cheerleader with soft blonde hair and porcelain skin who made my heart stop because, as we danced at St. Tolentine's one spring night, she asked me, "What's your name?" in perfect harmony to the lyrics of the slow song that we danced to. After her, there was a girl who reminded me of Grace Kelly. She was aristocratic and intelligent. I fell in love with her bearing and sensibility. Then there was little dark-haired Sheila and the practical, motherly Eileen. With each of them, my desire to unlock the mysteries of sex undoubtedly made me a selfish and inconsiderate partner. But I suspect that experience had taught those girls not to expect much of young men in the way of maturity or sensitivity.

So I was drawn toward manhood, desperately wanting to be an adult sexually, but frantically wishing that the years would slow so that I would not have to face the reality of Vietnam. Most of my friends entered senior year of high school dreaming about college, not only as a four-year escape from the rules and regulations of Catholic discipline but also as a stay against the draft and entry into the war.

We treated our last year in high school like a final party before a big exam. I continued working at Kohlman Hall alongside my friend Dennis Murphy, who worked in the kitchen assisting the cook. One Monday I came to work and was interrogated by Brother Hagen, who had just fired Dennis. He had come upon Dennis sitting outside Kohlman Hall after work on Friday, waiting for Chris Young to pick him up in his 1955 Cadillac. The problem for Brother Hagen was what Dennis was sitting on: three cases of beer that he had taken from the basement storage area. Once I convinced Brother Hagen that I hadn't been pilfering all along with Dennis— who, as I found out later, had been taking cigarettes and beer for some time—he let me stay on. But it wasn't much fun without Dennis's sly smile and ever-present sarcasm. Besides, I don't think Brother Hagen was ever really convinced that I wasn't part of some large cigarette- and beer-smuggling gang, with Dennis as its ringleader. I began to see Brother Hagen's red crewcut everywhere I went—the kitchen, the washroom, the basement—and to hear the swish of his robes behind me in every corridor. He became as ubiquitous as Mr. Marcelonis, but never as interesting.

In the spring of that year, Dennis, Kevin Flynn, and I often jumped in someone's car and headed out to Rockaway Beach. We would spend Friday night in Fitzgerald's Bar on 108th Street. It was small and crowded with young people; the smell of beer and Scotch filled our noses, cigarette smoke burned our eyes and throats, and the voices rose around us like sounds in a dream.

On any weekend in the spring Kevin Flynn and I might find ourselves at 3:00 A.M. on the wind-chilled beach, after we had found a girl, made out on the boardwalk, and returned to the bar to discover that everyone was gone—that there were no rooms to stay in, and that all of our friends' cars seemed to have disappeared. Then Kevin and I would end up on the sand, near the edge of the boardwalk, between two trash cans, the cold drilling into our bones. We were two seventeen-year-old boys who would never touch another male for fear that we would be considered "queer," but on those nights, when the cold made our joints ache, we fell into a fetal sleep and pressed against one another until the sun rose and we sprang apart with a bleary-eyed awkwardness.

During the long, dreamy afternoons after such nights, I would lie on the grey sand of Rockaway, inhaling the rich salt air, gazing at the girls who sat around me glistening with baby oil, and wondering what would come next. Looking obliquely into the sun-dazzled waves, I dreamt of Holden Caulfield and Percy Bysshe Shelley and Christopher Columbus. Portia's lines from *The Merchant of Venice* played in my head. I planned my exit from the Bronx, realizing that I wanted not my due, not justice from the world, but mercy, which I knew even then was probably just another form of luck and never really something that anyone deserved.

I always had a book with me. In the late spring of 1967 it was *Catch-22*. Toward the end of May, on my last excursion to Rockaway on a Saturday afternoon after one of those raucous Friday nights and bone-aching and restless early morning sleeps, I read the last lines of that novel: "Yossarian jumped. Nately's whore was hiding just outside the door. The knife came down, missing him by inches, and he took off."

It made me want to run, even though I didn't have a clear idea from what—the war in Vietnam, the stifling rules at Mount St. Michael, my father's sadness, the dark stolidity of the Bronx itself.

The world I wanted to run to had beautiful women, clear, open skies, and a never-ending stream of books. Or perhaps, I thought, it is something different from anything I can visualize, but I must keep my eyes open so that I will recognize my good fortune when I sight it. As I closed *Catch-22* and shut my eyes against the sun, I dreamt that I, along with Yossarian, was heading toward that place.

.....

Richard Tricario's face has widened around the jowls, and his eyes are a bit shadowed, but these changes have only added to a look of pleasant hound-dog handsomeness. He has the hint of a smile in his eyes and around his lips, as if he is ready to laugh at any moment. "Just give me a good reason," his expression seems to say. His hair, now steel gray and thinning, is still oiled back into a modest pompadour. He still smokes unfiltered Camels, and his voice, like a rake scraping over cobblestones, compels attention and adds a texture to his gentleness.

It is the spring of 1995, and we are standing in the quadrangle, now filled with parked cars, as we talk about the new Bronx, the present Mount St. Michael. It seems that it's not safe anymore to park a car on the streets near the school. It's not even safe to ride the city buses. "We had to buy a whole fleet of buses," Tricario tells me, "because the kids were getting mugged and beat up on their way to school in the mornings." The school, like the Bronx, has changed in the past twenty-five years. Now, half the students are Black and Hispanic, many are from single-parent families, a good number are not Catholic, and some don't go on to college. "Our students have a much wider range of abilities than they did when you were here," he says. "We send kids to Harvard *and* Bronx Community College. Twenty-five years ago just about everyone went to a good four-year school."

Somehow, I'm surprised that Tricario is still teaching, not because I thought the job would have worn him out, but because I thought he would be far past retirement age by now. Looking up at him as a teenager, I assumed he was already middle-aged, but when I was a freshman, he had just recently graduated from Iona College, and as an experiment on his way to his real goal of becoming an FBI agent he had taken a job teaching. The experiment had transformed him, though, and now in his midfifties he is one of the top administrators in the school.

Times have changed, he tells me. "You can't rap kids on the head any more to get their attention." But as we tour the buildings, and he stops to answer students' questions, I notice that the same easy smile creases his rough face and the same humor edges along each word he speaks. In the cafeteria he walks up to one young man, taps him lightly on the head, and reminds him to pick up an application in his office that afternoon. Another young man comes up to him and asks to speak with him after school. When the student walks away, Tricario explains to me that the young man transferred early in the fall from Evander Childs High School. Just a few weeks ago, Mount St. Michael received a transcript of the student's work that showed passing grades in a number of classes the student had never taken because he transferred. "That tells you something about public high schools in New York City," Tricario says. "Theoretically, that young man could have graduated without ever attending the school."

We stroll into the teachers' dining room, and he introduces me to Jim Chambers. I knew him thirty years ago as Brother Bruce, the principal of St. Philip Neri. I would never have recognized him, and not because the coal-black hair has turned to strips of silver. He seems too shy and innocent to be the keen-eyed man I knew as Brother Bruce. Outside the cafeteria, in the quadrangle, I look up at the window I used to gaze down from when I was watching for

Charley Patrick. When I tell Tricario the story, I'm pleased to hear him say, "He was a strange one, all right." It confirms for me that the past was real, that even if Brother Bruce has changed his name and left some boldness behind with my memory of him, Charley Patrick was perhaps as unblinkingly stern as I recall. It is heartening to discover that the past is not an illusion to which we obstinately cling. The past is real. It is always there, a landscape to be rediscovered, renamed. My dreams of getting out of the Bronx have led me back to it, to Tricario, to the knowledge that in venturing out we must always bring with us what we think we leave behind.

For a few moments before I drive away, I sit in my car and observe the school. It is like peering into a crack that opens into the past and the present. Two young men stand on the edge of the track, the goal posts and classrooms beyond them. Their ties blowing in the breeze, the brick towers and turrets behind them, they stand alone, facing one another, immersed in their conversation, not realizing that I'm watching them and imagining the years disappearing until they are the ones looking back, trying to remember what was real and what imagined. Even though I can't see him anymore, I know Richard Tricario is still in the quadrangle just the other side of the tree line at the far end of the oval track, that he is about to enter the main building to continue his day, a day no more tangible, no more real than the ones I remember from the receding past.

....

PART THREE

Voyage

Mad voyage has its appeal.

—Josephine Humphries,
The Fireman's Fair

*To arrive where we started and know the place for the
first time.*

—T. S. Eliot, "Little Gidding"

CHAPTER 6

Fordham University
and Ground Zero

He'd been lugging around Miss MacIntosh for years.
It had the advantage of being plotless, as far as he
could tell, but invariably interesting, so he could dip
into it at random.
　　　　　—Anne Tyler, *The Accidental Tourist*

But as the Edsel took off, spavined and sprung, sunk
at one corner and flatulent in its muffler, spuriously
elegant and unsound, . . . a final question did occur
to him and he took off after it.
　　　　　—Walker Percy, *The Last Gentleman*

And he thought again of Venus combing and
combing her hair as she drifted through the Bronx.
　　　　　—John Cheever, "The Country Husband"

Although I didn't read *Miss MacIntosh, My Darling* until many years later, I met Marguerite Young when I was a sophomore at Fordham University. Her classes were like her prose—dreamy and uneventful. One session would just float into another for no appar-

ent reason, but like dreams, they haunted me with a meaning beyond my grasp. There was something of the phantasm about Miss
Young herself. Even now, as I recall her sitting at her desk in front
of our creative writing class, she seems odd enough to be a figment
of my imagination. She was one of the homeliest women I have
ever seen, with stringy, colorless hair cut into blunt, uneven bangs
that one semester rose high on her lined forehead and the next
hung into her sad, swollen eyes. The very fact of gravity was detailed in her face. The flesh hung loose everywhere, blanched as if it
had never seen the daylight. The bags under her eyes sagged into
her large nose, and her jowls reached like flaps toward her wrinkled neck. Her thin lips nearly always had an unfiltered cigarette
dangling from them. She would sit at her desk, looking out from
her deep, dark eyes at us, as an ash gathered precariously and dan-
gled over her papers. I sometimes found it impossible to concentrate on anything she might be saying because I became hypnotized
by the growing ash and the tiny stream of saliva that invariably
began to course down the groove of flesh where her jowls met her
wide chin. Even then, at nineteen years old and in awe of most of
my professors, I felt a strange distance from her, as if she were not
so much a real person as something I had conjured. She was a
writer, the first one I had encountered in the flesh, and her exotic appearance didn't disappoint my imagination. She seemed as gentle
as some alien creature, never unkind but somehow unhuman, or
perhaps too human. I felt that there was something serene and
something frightening about her at the same time. For me, she was
Miss Havisham and Emily Brontë, both imagined and real, both
dark illusion and strange reality.

I loved her class and her too, though, for she made me believe
in my own dream life. She was more fantastic than most of the people I had met up to that point inside the classroom or out of it. She
smoked and coughed her way through each class. On rainy days

she would wear a clear plastic raincoat to school, and eventually she seemed to like that attire so much that she took to wearing it even on sunny days. She lived on Bleecker Street in Greenwich Village, in an apartment next to a Hungarian princess in a building on the site where Herman Melville was born, she told us, and she often had dreams in which Henry James visited her like some Dickensian apparition and engaged her in literary discussions. After a few weeks in her course I went out and found a used paperback copy of her first and only novel, the twelve-hundred-page *Miss MacIntosh, My Darling*, which Scribner's published in 1965. In 1947 Miss Young had signed a contract for the book with Maxwell Perkins, the legendary editor for Hemingway, Fitzgerald, and Thomas Wolfe. She had planned to finish the book in two years. Perkins died the same year he signed the contract with her, and it took her seventeen more to finish the novel. In class she took pride in telling us that the work had been compared to Joyce's, and, like *Finnegans Wake*, had taken nearly two decades to write. I'm not sure if she assumed, as Joyce seemed to, that her readers should take an equal amount of time to read her masterpiece. It took me longer, about a quarter of a century to read beyond page twenty-six. Like Macon Leary in Anne Tyler's *The Accidental Tourist*, I carried the book with me, slipping in and out of it like a recurring dream.

When I met her, Marguerite Young was approaching sixty, but she seemed more ancient to me than any person I had ever encountered. And more alien. It was not difficult for me to imagine her in Greenwich Village communing with Herman Melville or Henry James, but I found it impossible to see her born and raised, as she was, in Indianapolis, Indiana, or going to school at Indiana University in Bloomington. A picture of her discussing Hume or Cervantes with a Hungarian princess made sense to me, but the image of her strolling the sun-bleached streets of Bloomington seemed wrong. She was too exotic to be a product of Middle America, too ethereal to be part of the world in which I found myself in 1968. But, perhaps, her subject was always America, the dreaming American mind. In one of her essays, "The Middle West of Everywhere," she wrote: "The Middle West is probably a fanatic state of mind. It is, as I see it, an unknown geographic terrain, an amorphous substance, the ghostly interplay of time with space, the cosmic, the psychic, as near to the North Pole as to the Gallup Pole. . . . I am in love with whatever is eccentric, devious, strange, singular, unique, out of this world. . . . From my point of view, America has not yet been discovered in that romantic light which is a conspiracy of poetry, history, philosophy."

For her, I wrote stories of my own dreams, of Vietnam and Canada. For her I wrote my first story after I graduated from high school, "The Time is Out of Joint," about a young man who is drafted and sent to Vietnam, and who dreams of a trip he took to Canada when he was contemplating dodging his fate. But, with heartfelt allusions to *Hamlet* and innocent appropriations of Ambrose Bierce, I had the sad young man, used by fate and his own inability to act decisively, killed by a Vietcong bullet just as his dream of escape reaches a climax. Miss Young had faith enough in my potential to try to persuade me to become a writer when I told her that I planned to get a license to teach in the New York City public schools. Then, her advice seemed impossible, like running off to join the circus. My world was populated by construction workers and bus drivers. Becoming a school teacher seemed leap enough into another world. Becoming a writer seemed a step onto a different planet, into some "fanatic state of mind."

In her class, though, I was in a different world. "Read your story to us, Mr. Pearson," she would say, her voice a soft rustling. She would tilt her head upward and close her eyes. Her head would stay at that angle throughout the reading. When it was done, she would open her eyes slowly, as if she were reluctantly reentering the physical world. Then she would smile, an unfocused, wrinkled smile, and place another cigarette between her moist lips.

When other people read their stories, I'd watch her mournful face and wonder if she had drifted into her own immense dream, her sprawling fiction, peopled with the phantasmic characters Mr. Spitzer, Esther Longtree, or Vera Cartwheel. I imagined that she was hearing her own breathless prose from *Miss MacIntosh, My Darling:*

> Not strange that, through the many years spent with the dreaming opium lady, Mr. Spitzer should know of the subterranean world—of the vast unconscious like a dream no one had dreamed—of the sea's transmutations—of places with golden spires and red roofs sunken under the whirling sea—of narrow queens with wooden faces—of bloated kings with red cheeks, their gold curls wired with silver wires—sunken harps, galleons in flooded drawing rooms, gleamings of silver and gold fins and great fish eyes shaped like race-tracks—brazen-footed horses with manes of flowing gold, manes streaking the waters like the dying sunset—old heroes nurtured on a diet of mare's milk—babes at the breasts of the mare mothers—the sea's burning gold—birds with steeple heads and wings as wide as bronze church doors.

For Marguerite Young, the Bronx seemed to be no more than an opium dream. She floated through it on her way back to Greenwich Village, listening to the voices she heard, the characters she saw in her visions. For me, the Bronx was more substantial than her conjurings, and I felt held by its limits.

But as I careened my way through 1968 and 1969, her advice to me confirmed some deep intuition I had about myself. It lay there inside of me, and I carried it with me like *Miss MacIntosh, My Darling*, waiting to be read. Just as it took me many years to read her whole story, it took me many years to believe her suggestion, to listen to her hoarse, dream-weighted voice calling to me.

During those two years in particular, the world seemed to explode, and I felt as if I were always at ground zero. In 1968 the world was a battleground. In Vietnam we fought an enemy tunneled underground. In America the battle was in the streets, the Black Panthers getting gunned down and arrested, the Weathermen bombing buildings in big cities, the police clubbing young people on the main avenues of Chicago. Each night the television showed pictures of burning cities and white-helmeted police officers wildly wielding batons, cracking skulls. The conversation in the bars, on the street corners, and around the dinner table was about the war in Vietnam and the protests in America. The images on television and in the newspapers were of young men who resembled me, their faces contorted in anger, facing men who like my father were in hard hats. They were not fathers and sons, but they could have been us—we looked so much alike.

On April 4, 1968, Martin Luther King, Jr. was shot as he stood on a motel balcony in Memphis, Tennessee. The Blacks in the inner cities went mad with grief. Buildings were set ablaze, and people were killed. The spring of my freshman year, in my philosophy class at Fordham University, we sat in a circle and discussed the meaning of the violence. All of us were White, including the instructor, and some students in the class expressed disapproval of the response to King's death. It was the first time I had ever seen a teacher show real anger at his students because of their ideas and not merely for some misbehavior. He made me feel shallow because I did not understand fully the desire to tear down the world that had destroyed Martin Luther King, Jr. I remember that the professor canceled our class in disgust and told us to go home and think about what we had lost. It was the first time that I was made to feel shame over what the world had *not* taught me, but it was also one of the first times that a teacher made me feel that my response to the world was more important than how well I performed on a test or how carefully I followed the rules. From that moment on, school became far less elegant than geometry, but much more important.

Martin Luther King, Jr.'s death lingered in my mind, and like Kennedy's assassination, it was played over and over again in the media. Kennedy's murder was no longer an aberration. Many of us began to wonder if it were simply the way of the world, a seething anger and hatred that just needed a spark to set it off. In the ensuing weeks, federal troops guarded the White House, there were riots in more than one hundred American cities, more than twenty thousand people were arrested, and dozens of people died. Then three months later our worst fears were confirmed: the world we lived in was rotten to its very core. I was a few weeks from my nineteenth birthday when Robert Kennedy was shot down just as he appeared to be succeeding in his attempt to get the Democratic nomination to run for president. Later in that summer, when the plot of the Democratic National Convention in Chicago offered only one ugly protagonist, Mayor Richard Daly, many of us felt lost. There were no more Kennedys to save us. The future was filled with the good-intentioned but gross Lyndon Johnson and, worse, the graceless and false Richard Nixon.

We turned inward. And we turned toward one another, hoping, I think, to find some meaning in each other that the world of our parents could no longer offer. College was a safe haven. As the world crashed down around me, college gave me sanctuary from the draft and a way of dreaming myself out of the Bronx. Fordham University campus was in the center of the Bronx, but it seemed as far away from it as my thoughts. It seemed rich in its wisdom and deep in its silence. The buildings appeared aristocratic, older than the awkward brick buildings I saw every day. The discussions I heard on the library steps were not the conversations I listened to on the subway platforms. We argued over literature and film as we argued about the war in Vietnam. Each day I felt myself being made into something new, and I expected that one day when I stepped past the gate onto Southern Boulevard, the Bronx would be gone and another world would have taken its place.

Nobody demanded that I come to class, cut my hair, or wear a tie. Instead, I was asked to think about philosophy and science and literature. I read Camus and was stunned by *The Stranger*. All of my years of Catholic education were stripped bare before his questioning. I began to drift away from mass, missing now and then, eventually not going at all. Confession held a tighter grip on me, for now along with all my other sins I had my guilt for not attending church. Eventually, the voice of the priest in the confessional could no longer offer solace or understanding. Only writers could. I read John Fowles's *The Magus* and felt close to the labyrinthine mystery at its heart. I wrote to Fowles about the novel, and he answered my letter, making me feel as if we shared a story, a way of being in the world. I read Vonnegut and Kesey and Brautigan, anyone who could show me a world separate from but similar to the one I saw every day.

In my freshman year, I remember the excitement I felt on the first day of Father O'Grath's philosophy class when the burly, red-cheeked professor said, "Before this semester is finished, I will prove to each and every one of you in this room that, without question or doubt, God exists." Caught, as I felt I was, between the sacraments and a gaping hole in the universe, I was pleased to hear such news. I was old enough to know better, I suppose, but deep inside I wanted to believe not only that Father O'Grath was going to provide detailed proof of God's existence—splinters of the cross, shards of the Decalogue, brittle fragments of burnt bushes—but that he might actually have more immediate proof. A tape-recorded message? A faded photograph? For the next few weeks of class, as we discussed Socrates, Aristotle, Plato, Epicureanism and Skepticism, Augustine and Pascal, Scholasticism and Materialism, I waited. Finally, the day arrived, and Father O'Grath stood before us with the requisite bulk, it seemed to me, to summon God or to cart in the necessary evidence to prove His existence. It didn't take me long to realize, though, that he planned to prove that God existed by discussing the nature of semantics and analytic philosophy. With great enthusiasm and humor he discussed the nature of syllogisms:

> God is love.
> Love is blind.
> Ray Charles is blind.
> Ray Charles is God.

For a moment I wondered, "Is that it? All these years of Catholic education have led to this surprise? That Ray Charles is really God?" I liked Ray Charles well enough and could even have imagined him as the secretary of the interior, but as God? I realized that Father O'Grath was happy to treat this syllogism as an interesting intellectual puzzle to be solved, while I felt like a man who had slipped through the ice of a frozen pond being asked by his rescuers to diagram a compound sentence. As the class proceeded, I realized that Father O'Grath was never going to produce physical evidence, let alone God Himself, and all I would hear would be intricate arguments that finally came down to one statement—"If God were possible, then He must exist, for He is the essence of all possibility." I left the room wishing Ray Charles *were* God, or at least wishing he were giving a concert on campus that weekend.

In general, though, college made me feel alive in a world that reeked with the possibility of death. I read all of Shakespeare in Mr.

Palven's class and the American novelists in Mr. Loprete's. The darker the world outside the campus, the more illuminating my studies became. I tried to use the stories and ideas from literature and philosophy to light my way into the world. Sometimes those stories helped to clarify my experience, and sometimes they left me dazed by the discrepancy between the two.

I read Shirley Jackson's "The Lottery" in the fall of 1969, shortly after Nixon proposed a major reorganization of the draft. I read it as I rode the train to Toronto, where I was going to speak with men who had left the country rather than enter the service. I had never read the story before, as many had, in high school, and my college instructors had not assigned it, but I felt compelled to read it as I headed toward Canada. It seemed strange to me then that I had spent so much time thinking about leaving the Bronx, and now it was likely that the government would force me to go—not to the quiet shores of Long Lake in Naples, Maine, where I spent a week each summer as a child, or to San Francisco, which I longed to see, but to Vietnam. For a long time, getting out of the Bronx had meant a new life; now, leaving had a terrifying finality to it. The world, like Shirley Jackson's story, had a nightmarish reality, an odd, illogical quality that made it seem like a dream in which I was wide awake.

In Jackson's story, the villager who chose the paper with a black dot on it was stoned to death by townspeople, friends, and family. There seemed to be no rhyme or reason to the execution, just as there seemed to be no logic in who would be chosen on December 1 to fight in Vietnam. The only difference between Jackson's lottery and the one that the U.S. government had instituted was that the U.S. lottery had more black dots, more chances to lose. As I walked the streets of Toronto, the last lines of Jackson's story—" 'It isn't fair, it isn't right,' Mrs. Hutchinson screamed, and then they were upon her."—echoed in my mind along with the last sentence of

Nixon's message about the new draft proposal—"We should do no less for the youth of our country." Each sentence seemed equally weighed down with irony.

During the trip to Toronto I felt as if I were sleepwalking. The blazing fall landscape of New York State had already chilled to a somber brown. The sky was an unending grey tunnel as the train shook and rattled up to Lake Ontario and along its shoreline into a wintry Canada. The young men I met at the Draft Resisters Coalition were not fervent revolutionaries, but nineteen year olds whose eyes were undistinguished, even weary and unfocused. As I spoke to them, I felt as if I were gazing into a steamy mirror and seeing nothing more remarkable than the vague outlines of my own confused expression.

I made no decisions about the draft during my two-day stay in Toronto. I just waited for December 1. Oddly enough, as important as that night was to me, I didn't stay home as many of my friends did to watch Representative Alexander Pirnie reach into a large glass bowl and pull out a blue capsule, open it, and read the first date—September 14. Instead, I was playing basketball at P.S. 8. Perhaps I assumed that I would get home in time to see the drawing on television or hear it on the radio. Perhaps playing basketball, the order and physical beauty of it, seemed the best response I could find to such a random, inexplicable universe. The game was both a physical release and an entry into a logical world of cause and effect. It was a syllogism that I could understand. There was no God in it, nor was any necessary. Perhaps I just didn't want to think at all, but instead to move and run, even if the movement led nowhere in particular. I recall walking into the cold night, the sweat cooling on my face, my warm skin turning brittle, and the chill as I remembered that my life was changed, but I didn't know yet in what way. By the time I got home at 9:45, the drawing was complete, and although the news announced the first few birth dates chosen and the last date, number 366, June 8, I had no idea where June 18 fell in the order of chance.

At about 10:30 I called up Dennis Murphy, and he told me, sadly, that my number was 12. We exchanged a few mumbled curses, and I spent that evening in my bed with my eyes open and my thoughts on my bleak future. The next morning, I picked up a copy of the *New York Times* and saw that my number was actually 341. That meant my chances of being drafted were virtually nonexistent. When I called Murph about it, he said, "Aw, shit, I was only kidding." I said, "Fuck you," and hung up on him, but I really didn't hold it against him because that sort of joke was typical of the way my friends communicated with one another. Rarely did we exchange a serious word. We spent our lives jostling one another, elbowing and slapping, teasing, "sounding" any perceived weakness. Sarcasm was as natural as breathing the sallow air of the Bronx. Besides, I had been released. After the lottery, I didn't have to leave the Bronx, allowing my desire to rise within me.

After December 1, 1969, the war became a moral and philosophical problem for me, not a tangible, physical one. The sky over the Bronx still had a yellowish tint to it, but it didn't seem as ominous or as pervasive as it had for the past few years. The world was not fair, I realized, but it went on anyway after the lottery. I felt like one of Camus's characters, free now to choose in an absurd situation. But while I pondered what choices to make, even what questions to ask, my ordinary life continued, even as the war thundered off stage. On the weekends my friends and I gathered at one of the bars on Bedford Park Boulevard, usually at Darby O'Gill's.

Darby's was typical of those bars in the Bronx in the late 1960s or even now, for that matter. It stood in the shadow of the church. It was dark, almost cavelike, and the air was moist with beer and disappointment. Old men sat along the back of the bar, hunched over boilermakers, laconic and heavy lidded. As the night went on, those men invariably became more talkative, more lachrymose, as if the moisture in the bar loosened some rusted hinge in their memory. Young men stood near the front door, leaning against the barstools, talking and waiting for the night truly to begin. Every now and again there was an ironic exchange between a twenty year old and one of the older men, but most often there was a wall of silence between the two groups, as if the older ones didn't want to recall their past and the younger ones were afraid to acknowledge what might be their future. Occasionally, someone like the thirty-year-old Dennis Cunningham would enter the bar, and everyone, young and old alike, would greet him with a mixture of genuine and contrived exuberance. Dennis was a bit slow, and for that he was both mocked and loved because his innocence made him both an object of derision and envy.

Attention would swing from Dennis to Rip and then to someone else, but by ten o'clock or so the young men were ready to leave, ready for the evening to begin in earnest. Usually, on Friday nights my friends and I would head toward Fordham University's Ramskeller. We would spend the evening there drinking beer, making a pyramid of empty paper cups on our table, occasionally going out to smoke some pot, and then returning to dance with some long-haired young women in bell-bottoms and capes.

On those weekend nights we may have forgotten what we were seeking, or perhaps we found exactly what we wanted—to lose ourselves in a buzz of drink and music and dance. For the first time in our lives we had begun to consider what our lives meant. For the first time in our lives we began to discuss politics, morality, our dreams for the future. But the old ways and the old neighborhood died hard, and the old fear of seriousness lingered. So, although we may have been able to talk about the war with some solemnity, we still seemed unable to speak about girls or being in love. We were masters of discussing the female anatomy, experts with just a minimum of experience, but when it came to speaking of our feelings about girls, we were struck dumb. And we often acted dumb as well.

I remember one of the first nights we went to the Ramskeller in my freshman year. More than a half dozen of us came over from Darby's. Frankie Bartoletti, Chris Young, Dennis Murphy, Steve Tarnok, Al Arater, Rip, and someone that Frankie knew from the days at Mount St. Michael, Robert Gentino. Early in the evening I met a young woman named Elaine, a student at Manhattan College. She had ivory skin, a soft voice, and wrists so thin they made your heart ache. I spent the evening talking and dancing with her as my friends roamed the room like a group of wild dogs. Every now and again I heard their barking laughter as they swept by me. When the evening was drawing to a close and I had said goodnight to Elaine, I walked outside the Ramskeller to find my friends. They were at the top of the stairs, shouting at a group of girls who obviously had not returned some demonstration of affection my drunken friends had offered with all the charm and dignity they could muster. When one of the girls, a blond with freckles and lively blue eyes, turned and said, "Get lost," as if she meant it, Gentino turned his pebbled face away from them and dropped his pants. He didn't have the good manners to show only his rear but twirled to show a front view, which included his pockmarked face as well as his penis. The girls, a bit of fright added to their disgust, rushed out into the night air. Some of my friends laughed, but most of them quieted. They hadn't had so much to drink that some forms of stupidity couldn't sober them up a bit. They stood there silent or laughing, most of them embarrassed, and Chris Young even ran out into the night to apologize to the girls. Of course, when he returned, he made a joke about his apology, and we all laughed one last time before we headed home.

.....

There were many more nights at the Ramskeller or the Inwood Lounge or the Cheetah. Hardly any of those girls have names in my recollections of them now. They are just a blur of faces, different hair colors, various shapes. During my first year in college the rhythm of the week was taken up by school during the day, work at the telephone company each evening from four until eight, and then a long, lost, timeless weekend. I worked at the telephone company in upper Manhattan, across the Inwood Bridge from the Bronx, for two and a half years as an account representative. I worked with Chris Young, Dennis Murphy, Steve Tarnok, Al Arater, Patty Dougherty, and a few others from the neighborhood in the Bronx. It was the perfect job for a college student, giving us the day for classes and the night for study. However, it didn't do much for our sense of social conscience. Essentially, we were collection agents, hired supposedly because we were organized and articulate.

The managers at the telephone company must have assumed that we had enough ambition to make us heartless as well. Our job was to check which accounts had not been paid, to send notices, and to follow up on the notices we had sent already. If we couldn't reach the person, we were to put in an order to shut off phone service. Some of my friends didn't even bother to call. They just put a note saying that they tried to contact the person and then canceled service. But others kept calling and calling throughout the shift, unable to write the order to snip the lines on some elderly woman's or welfare mother's phone. Some of my friends kept putting the slips in the back of the pile so that certain phones stayed on for weeks and weeks after no payment was received. We came in each afternoon to the condescending glances of some of the full-time workers, who saw us, I think, as college boys who were going to have things too easy in life. We sat alongside them at their desks, at the mercy of their peripheral vision until five o'clock, when most of them left. Then we were on our own. In a desultory manner we went about our work for the next few hours, getting enough done to satisfy our supervisors, but spending most of our time hanging out with one another as if it were just another night at Darby O'Gill's. Dennis often headed to the lounge to make long-distance calls, and rather than feeling moral indignation, I was depressed that I knew no one outside my local calling area.

It was the late 1960s, the war raged on television and in the newspapers, college kept deepening our awareness of a larger world than the one measured between Fordham Road and Bedford Park Boulevard, and most of us sensed, I'm certain, that other places waited, expecting us to arrive at any moment. We didn't get far in those college years. We were middle class, at best, and never even thought of such things as a year of study abroad. I had a scholarship to Fordham, but there were still bills to pay. Most of my friends needed to save for their tuition. We were coming to a sense of ourselves intellectually and emotionally at a time when the consensual wisdom had it that young people were breaking with every tradition—economically, sexually, politically. But, although we were shaped by the times in deep and lasting ways, most of us plodded along like good Catholic boys, working at our part-time jobs, passing our courses, being respectful to our parents. Of course, when we were alone, we might take a tab of acid and listen to The Who wail "I'm Free," feeling the vibrations settle in the very nerves of our teeth. We might smoke a joint with our friends on a grassy knoll outside the Ramskeller on Friday night, passing it around and around, until only Jerome Mahon, his eyes burnt with streaks of red, would care to hold the damp fraction of burning paper between his thumb and index finger to get the last harsh smoke into his lungs. We grew our hair down to our shoulders, marched in candlelight vigils against the war, and argued angrily against our parents' vision of the good life. But we kept our jobs, and we did our calculus, no matter how much we hated both.

Like some of my friends, I wanted a new life, one that college and books were opening up for me, a life of study and contemplation, of achievement and wisdom, of adventure and unknown landscapes. What I got, though, was the phone company and, during the summer weekends, the Hamptons.

Each summer during my college years a group of us would rent a house near the beach in Hampton Bays, Southampton, or Quogue. Every weekend we would head east, out of the Bronx, and onto the Long Island Expressway for the trip past all the names we associated with suburbs, green lawns, and ranch houses—Hempstead, Babylon, Islip—toward the rich, funky smell of the sea air. Usually we left after school or work on Friday night and ended up as part of a long traffic jam, a slow slithering line of lights that extended for mile after mile on the expressway. If I were lucky, Al Arater had gotten a ride with me and sat in the back seat playing his guitar for a couple of hours until the traffic began to thin out when we reached Highway 27, the single-lane road that cut a straight line all the way out to Montauk.

On those weekends we tried to live some sort of fantasy life. During the day we spent our time on Hot Dog Beach, tossing a football, body surfing the waves, and drinking Bash, a deceptively sweet mixture of juices, beer, and any available hard liquors. The Bash was generally mixed in a large plastic barrel by someone with hairy legs and a low forehead who had the kind of sense of humor that led him to drop socks, underwear, and pieces of lint into the mixture as he stirred it. Such drinking in the hot sun led to some terrible sunburns, some chipped teeth in the surf, and a few lost weekends. During our first summer renting a house, it wasn't uncommon for someone, after a night's drinking game, to wake up in the cold morning light, naked in the bathtub, with the shower dripping slowly on his aching forehead. Most often after that first summer of freedom, though, we showed more self-discipline, at least until darkness fell.

Then we would head out to Dune Road and spend the night dancing and desperately trying to join the sexual revolution. We all seemed to have a narrative sense, we told so many tall tales, but more often than not our rental house was filled at night with drunken young men too tired to fight over who got one of the three or four beds.

Of course, on a number of occasions young women did find their way into one of those houses. Dates always got the bedrooms. That meant that the best looking or the smoothest talking got special privileges; there may have been some hard feelings, but most of us realized that such a system was merely a reflection of how our society worked anyway. Therefore, the thick tongued and the homely just accepted their fate. It was like working for IBM or General Motors. We acknowledged the difference between the top executives and middle management. It was the sixties, but there was nothing of the commune about the group. And the community, such as it was, was not utopian, but bacchanalian. We lived for a tingling buzz brought on by liquor and pot and the sweet, briny smell of girls' flesh, the salt breeze mingling with the perfume on their tanned skin as they danced in The Castaways by the beach.

And we lived for the stories that we could tell afterward. Not private tales of conquests, although surely those were told, but group adventures that had the chance of being turned into legends by the following weekend, stories that could be told in a communal voice, each speaker adding a twist to the plot. "Do you remember her father walking into the house at three in the morning?" someone would start it off. Then the story would circle the room, a story about the weekend that four girls spent the night. When another young woman's father showed up, everyone feigned sleep as he called her name in a slight German accent, the high beams from his car shining into the living room windows. Eventually, he came into the house and walked around the bodies strewn on the floor—wide awake but eyes shut tight, lips pressed together to suppress giggles as he called, "Jayne. Iss Jayne here?" She was out with one of my friends, but nobody was willing to step up from a feigned sleep to try to explain to an angry father who spoke with an accent what his daughter might be doing at such a time in the morning.

Or someone would say, "Were you here when Frankie and Maude were naked on the roof?"

"Do remember what Murphy looked like walking around in Claire's underwear?"

"I'll never forget Suane screaming out in the morning, 'Fuckin' Young.' He didn't even have to ask who put peanut butter in his ears the night before."

Some of the stories created their own stories, like expanding circles. Supposedly, Suane got his revenge on Young by making him a scotch and water that he mixed with the most private swizzle stick he could find on his person. After Patty Dougherty learned that Chris Young had stuffed peanut butter in Dennis Suane's ears as he lay unconscious in one of the bedrooms one night and that Suane had returned the favor by making him a scotch with pubic hair, Patty never again for the rest of the summer slept with both eyes closed, and he never touched his lips to a drink he didn't pour himself. Whatever time you passed by the spot where Patty slept, you'd see him there, a cyclops ready to spring into a defensive posture. If anyone offered him a drink, his eyes narrowed into ferocious slits. For the rest of the summer he always appeared to be dazed and snarling, which gave a perfect circularity to our stories, a connectedness, a sense that our paranoia and practical jokes all meant something. What, we weren't sure.

But something. And like Patty we waited for something else to happen.

In our legends, Maude seemed to slide from the roof to the backseats of cars, to ponds and blueberry bushes. She ended up anywhere the lure of offbeat sexual anecdote could take her, as if, like Rip, she was transformed and continuously re-created by the alluring narrative of our stories. With each story, Bartoletti became more fastidious and Murphy more unkempt. It was as if the stories created us. As we told these stories about each other and ourselves, we began to dream ourselves into significance.

It was as if with these stories we tracked our lives, perceived ourselves as unfinished fictional characters. All we needed was the right, exaggerated plot, and we could slip away from the stale air of the Bronx forever, from the specter of war, from sad jokes and dull jobs. I suspect that we were all looking for some dramatic change, something that would tell us how we were meant to live.

I fell in love with Jo-Ellen Kiernan the first time I saw her, although I didn't know it at the time. I was eighteen, and it was the fall of my freshman year of college. I had gone with Chris Young to watch his girlfriend, Jayne, in a musical play at her school, the Academy of the Sacred Heart of Mary. There on the stage, alongside Jayne, was a pretty young woman with very short blonde hair, heartbreakingly blue eyes, and such long, beautiful legs that I forgot to watch the rest of the play. I didn't get to meet her until weeks later at the Ramskeller. Jo-Ellen and I have slightly different memories of that night (we've had twenty-seven years to discuss it), but in essence we agree that we danced and talked for the entire evening, and I took her home. I recall, however, that our first dance was a slow one, and as I held her in my arms, she looked up at me with a far-away smile, then kissed me in a way I was not soon, ever actually, to forget.

We dated off and on over the next year. She had recently moved with her family from an apartment in the Highbridge area of the Bronx near Yankee Stadium to the second floor of a two-family house on Elm Place, a few blocks east of Webster Avenue, near Fordham University. A few weeks after I met her, I went to her house with my friend Steve Tarnok on a morning after a night-long snowfall. Joyful to be off from school on a weekday, Jo-Ellen's brothers played happily, dashing in and out of the hallway that connected the various rooms. Jo-Ellen, her sister Christine, and her mother were in the kitchen, which was at the far end of the house. We spent the morning drinking hot chocolate and talking. Jo-Ellen's mother was tall, imposing, and funny—outspoken, sometimes intentionally outrageous. Steve sat on the radiator next to the kitchen window, still open because Jo-Ellen's mother had just put out the wash. The window overlooked a clothesline that stretched across the backyard, a small rectangle of ground now filled with three feet of still-white snow. Jo-Ellen's mother began to tease Steve, who teased her back until she walked over to him and said, "It looks like I'll have to push you out the window." Which she did. He dropped about ten feet but onto a soft cushion of snow. Both Steve and I were impressed. He lay there with snow on his pointed nose, and I stood in the kitchen, my open mouth shaping itself into a grin. Jo-Ellen had a mother unlike any we had come to know, a mother who would push someone out a window. It didn't matter that she pushed Steve into the cold safety of the snow. It mattered that she did something so unexpected of a parent. It was a good sign, I thought, to be dating a beautiful young woman who had a mother like that. It suggested that life might hold all sorts of surprises.

Of course, at eighteen I wasn't smart enough to recognize some forms of good fortune. Instead, I worried about all those girls whom I could still meet, and my eyes often scanned the horizon. But, besides being beautiful, Jo-Ellen was patient, and by the end of my sophomore year I saw deeply enough into her eyes to know that it would be impossible to discover a deeper or more lasting mystery. During the summers of my sophomore and junior years, we went to the Hamptons together. Often, in the early morning we would find ourselves on the fog-shrouded beach, submerged in the ebb and flow of sound, surrounded by the wind. In the distances, north and south, the mist made the beach a ghostly nowhere, and to the east the ocean was a grey puzzle, a sighing, unanswered question. During the summer of my junior year in college as I was trying once again unsuccessfully to push my way through *Miss MacIntosh, My Darling*, I came across this line describing Miss Mac-Intosh's view of the world: "Old earth was simply good enough for her." When I looked into Jo-Ellen's eyes, I saw them focused on me and felt as if I were looking into my own future, and then, like Miss MacIntosh, I felt the world I inhabited was all I'd ever need, that even the Bronx was illuminated by possibility.

In a cabin overlooking Long Lake in Naples, Maine, as we lay on a bed in the pine- and dust-scented second-story room, Jo-Ellen and I talked about getting married and going to school in San Francisco. That lake, with all its memories of youthful dreams, led me to her. So it seemed fitting to me that during the week we spent there together, I often saw the dark blue water reflected in her eyes. She smelled of pine needles and sunlight, and it seemed to me then, as it does now, that my life at that moment became clear and whole. The evening breezes that riffled the lake and floated through the tree tops whispered to me that the fate I sought had found me.

We didn't get married until I graduated from college the following June. In the spring of my senior year I took courses in education at the Lincoln Center Branch of Fordham University and did my student teaching at Roosevelt High School in the Bronx in order to get my license to teach in New York State. I loved most of my classes, although I disliked my master teacher, a man who seemed more interested in taking attendance than in discussing literature. The more rapport I developed with my students, the more he seemed threatened by my presence in his room. I taught *One Flew Over the Cuckoo's Nest* and began to notice how much the school itself was like the hospital in the novel, with its metal fences and inmates and guards. As each day passed, my supervising teacher looked more like Nurse Ratched. He didn't think my tests contained enough objective questions; he thought we discussed the novel too much in class, that there should be more defining of *verisimilitude* and *allegory*; and he was absolutely opposed to the field trip we took to see an off-Broadway adaptation of the novel. He thought that the students might kill someone on the subway, but although they were far too loud, they injured no one, destroyed no property, and cheered enthusiastically when Chief Bromden escaped.

One student in that class, a sixteen-year-old girl with long brown hair and a body bursting the seams of a purple halter top and faded jeans shorts, sat next to me on the train as it rasped its way out of Manhattan and back into the Bronx. We talked a bit about McMurphy and why he didn't escape when he had the chance to go. She looked at me with soulful eyes and changed the subject as we leaned into one another as the train went into a dark curve.

"My parents don't understand me at all," she said.

I nodded and gave her a sympathetic look, tilting my head down to hear her above the lurching of the subway through a tunnel. I felt her warm breath on my neck, smelled her perfume, a scent of flowers, as it mixed with the burning metal of the train's wheels.

"I have a twenty-five-year-old boyfriend, and they don't understand." She leaned a bit closer to me. "I love to suck on . . ." The train screeched around another curve, the lights flickering, her bare leg pressing against mine. "I just like it . . . you know. I can't help it . . . if I like it, can I? What's the matter with that?"

She was very attractive, and she knew it. The question she was asking had another much more specific question behind it. I didn't give her much more than a mumbled, "Um, I see what you're saying," because I knew that I was a student teacher, twenty-one years old, and she was sixteen. I never gave her the answer I think she was looking for and perhaps the one that part of me wanted to offer. After I dropped the students off at Roosevelt High School, I took the bus home, thinking for a moment about her boyfriend, if there really was one, who was four years older than I was, and what after-school games they might have played when she was supposed to be studying vocabulary or memorizing world capitals.

On that bus ride home, past the crowds on Fordham Road and the old men playing checkers in Poe Park, past the older women dragging laundry carts behind them, past kids playing stickball on the side streets, past bricks and stoops and the dreamy stares of middle-aged women, their elbows braced against the sills and their fists knuckled against their cheeks, I rode with my forehead pressed against the grimy bus window and thought of Jo-Ellen and me, riding away from the Bronx on an adventure more exciting than any book I had read or story I could tell. I heard Marguerite Young's advice to me—"Don't get a license to teach in the public schools. Write. You should write. Ask yourself: what is it you really *have* to do?"—but I knew that as much as I took heart from her words, I could not listen fully to her final question. The Bronx was still too much a part of me to go too far. Mount St. Michael, my father's construction jobs, those delivery bikes were still there, only around the corner, and I couldn't forget them that easily.

In the winter of my senior year I saw Miss Young go into the subway at Webster Avenue and Fordham Road. I followed her down onto the platform, for a question had occurred to me, and in that instant I thought that she might be the only person I knew who could answer it. But I waited until the train came and then watched her get on, saw her sit down, her head framed in the window as the train clicked away. I never saw her again, but I wasn't disappointed that I had missed my chance to speak with her, for it dawned on me that there were actually two questions in my mind. One, Jo-Ellen had answered for me already, and the other, I realized, had a simple answer: "as long as it takes and wherever it takes you."

When I pushed open the doors of the subway station and returned to the afternoon light, I had my eyes on my fate, for I sensed that the lottery occurred each day, often quietly as we sleepwalked through our own lives. And I knew, when I felt Jo-Ellen's hand get entangled in mine, that I must be on the lookout not only for what would be treacherous, but for the strange and the beautiful as well. Such things were possible, I had learned, even under the dull skies of the Bronx.

·····

As part of my journey back to Fordham University I want to visit Marguerite Young, now eighty-seven years old, in her Bleecker Street apartment, but age has drawn her to Indiana, away from the spirits that inhabit her Greenwich Village flat, and back to her past, where she is being cared for by a niece. But I do get to speak with her on the telephone, a brief conversation, her voice scratching out phrases like a phonograph playing at a slow speed, a sound distant and worn.

"You don't remember me," I begin and tell her who I am and the advice she once gave me: be a writer. And how, at first, I could not follow it. I got married, had children, and did what I could while making other sorts of living.

"I remember you," she says. Her voice a whisper. A moan. "I remember you. You were lovely, a lovely writer. I remember your girlfriend. She was a sweetheart."

And for a moment I do believe that she remembers me and my stories and Jo-Ellen's face, all from twenty-five years ago, that a woman who could write *Miss MacIntosh, My Darling* might remember anything, whether it happened or not, that such precise memories might be part of her implacable, plotless genius. She had written an immense novel bursting with words, metaphor upon metaphor streaming forward like a river of dreams with its own irreversible, inexplicable logic.

When she says, "Call again," in a voice so gentle and far away that it is like the sound of a bittersweet memory itself, we both believe, perhaps, for an instant that such calls will be possible, that illness and death will accommodate our chance for reacquaintance. "I could teach you something still," she says, and, of course, I know she is right. But she is gone with the click and buzz of the phone and becomes once again one of the spirits of my past, leaving behind her river of words, words flowing into words, enough words to last a lifetime.

Buildings in the Bronx, near Fordham Road, rise up as if they wish to shove the reefs of clouds out of the way. The streets are crowded with people and cars flexing like the muscles of one great writhing body alongside piles of debris, plumes of smoke, graffiti, shouts, music, curses, laughter.

It takes my breath away, but I'm not sure if it's the exuberant, angry swelling of life or the simple lack of oxygen. Even in my childhood, Fordham Road was like this—honking, throbbing, grimy—but now it seems about to implode, to turn into its own dark center.

Fordham University now has gates and security guards to watch its borders, and once I walk onto campus, I see why. It is some other version of the Bronx, a pastoral of stone buildings and rolling hills—much the same as I recall it from the early 1970s, the smell of new-mown grass mingling with pipe smoke, students chattering as they walk the paths, professors smiling and nodding.

In Dealy Hall, Marguerite Young's office is now occupied by a young professor who talks to two students about "spiritual energy . . . God's power . . . a sense of communion." These are not phrases I hear often on my own campus. The Ramskeller is still there, but it is after the lunch hour and only a few students sit at the tables and in Hispanic accents discuss the O. J. Simpson trial, which is on the big-screen television set on the wall.

For a moment I linger on the steep marble steps of Keating Hall, the great stone turrets behind me, the parade grounds in front, and I realize that my boyhood in the Bronx was filled with towers and stone edifices as much as it was with brick apartment buildings and crowded streets. And it seems that all memory is mixed with longing—for the recollection to be clearer, sharper, filled with significance; for meaning not to get lost in the details of daily life; for the past to be as real as the present. When I close my eyes, what rises before me, though, are not towers, but faces and figures— Marguerite Young's, Vera Cartwheel's, Henry James's, Melville's— in a scene as surreal as one in *Miss MacIntosh, My Darling*. They are all waving, smiling, but it's difficult to tell if they are bidding me farewell or beckoning me home.

CHAPTER 7

Leaving *the* Bronx

As I watch the sun rise high over Fordham Road
Oh Mammy dear we're all mad over here
Livin' in America.
                    —Black 47, "Livin' in America"

Let's get outta the Bronx first.
                    —Richard Price, *The Wanderers*

I left the Bronx twice before I left it for good in 1971. Of course, I had taken trips before then, each summer for a week or so to Naples, Maine, or once to Florida and another time to Puerto Rico, but up until 1969 I never really left the Bronx behind me.

In the summer of 1969, after my sophomore year in college, the war pressed in on us from all sides. Nixon's lottery would not occur until December, freeing some of us from hard choices, but a good number of us felt trapped by place and time.

Therefore, in August 1969 I was ready to believe in a new country of tents and marijuana and mud in Bethel, New York, far away from Southeast Asia and, it seemed, far away from the Bronx as well. About twelve of us went to Woodstock, leaving the Bronx on a Friday afternoon, heading toward Sullivan County in upstate New

196

York. We had heard on the radio that the New York State Thruway had been shut down, an event that to us seemed as miraculous as Jesus's feat with the loaves and the fishes, and although most of us had by then given up going to mass and confession, religion had settled deeply in us, and the very miracle made us more determined to see what was going on in the Catskills. It was difficult to imagine that anything short of a nuclear war could force the thruway to close. Every young person in the Bronx seemed to have decided at the same instant that it was time to leave. Tens of thousands of cars lined the thruway, crammed with blank-eyed kids, their heads tilted as if they were listening to the same voice. It was a science-fiction movie without a spaceship, an exodus without a Moses.

We knew the area slightly because Jo-Ellen's parents had a summer house in Yulan, New York, about fifteen miles from Bethel. We skirted traffic by going through northern New Jersey, on the Palisades Parkway and then on the back roads until we reached Port Jervis, New York, a homely little railroad town right near the point where New York, New Jersey, and Pennsylvania all abut the Delaware River.

Route 97, the road that coils its way through the mountains to Yulan, winds through a scenic and scary stretch of road called the Hawk's Nest. We drove past the sheer cliffs and the view of the gurgling Delaware far below without making any conversation. I suspect that most of us were thinking about the last time we had been there—about two months before, after an impromptu trip to the mountains. We had decided to go in two cars, take an ounce of marijuana, and get a couple of motel rooms in the country, a bit north of Rip Van Winkle's dreamy territory, but in the same mountains. It didn't turn out to be a pastoral weekend.

I had spent the beginning of the summer reading *Trout Fishing in America, In Watermelon Sugar, Cat's Cradle, The Electric Kool-Aid*

Acid Test, and other books that led me toward a contemplation of the apocalypse and some dreamy-eyed, drug-related alternative to it. My friends might have been reading the same stuff because someone brought along a plastic bag filled with pot and a paper sack of assorted pills, snappers, papers, pipes, and other paraphernalia. Our reading led us, in some manner of homage to Brautigan and Wolfe and Vonnegut, to a form of laconic speech that seemed a strange blend of sarcasm and nonsequitur, of acceptance and the refusal to accept. *Yeah, right. Sure, Man.* Usually drawn out as if we had a speech impediment. *Maaaaaannn. Far out. Faaarrr oouut.* The phrase *far out* was a particularly popular one, for it could mean everything or nothing. It was the right phrase for both the poetic and the illiterate. The implications of *far out* could be comic or tragic. You could use it to suggest that you were listening carefully or that you were not listening at all. Besides, it implied other worlds, places distant and unfamiliar, places not the Bronx.

So as we headed into the exotic Catskills that weekend early in the summer, we all thought that we spoke the same language, that we knew what it meant to be "on the bus," and that without question we were. We reached the Catskills at dusk and found a motel on a shady hillside at the end of a long, winding road. When the darkness arrived, it seemed to come with a sudden desperation, a total blackness. We sat around talking and smoking the marijuana until we had smoked so much that our conversation became a repetitive chant—*Yeah, right. Sure, Maaann. FAR out.* What we lost in vocabulary, we searched for in inflection.

Everything seemed be to moving toward a quiet sort of anesthesia when one of my friends jumped up like a startled deer. In a frightened rush of words he said, "I can't take it anymore, I can't take it, I have to get out of here." With that said he rushed out of the motel room where we were all lying around, draped like old clothing over chairs and beds and table tops. He had a slight lisp, so it sounded to me as if he said, "I have to get out of fear." And when he ran out of the room, his words seemed to echo—"out of fear, fear, fear, fear." Everyone seemed to move in slow motion, through his words, but a few of us stumbled out to see what was the matter.

We found him outside in the darkness, and even in my haze I realized that his fear was not specific or localized. His terror was a general one. Of course, that made it all the more frightening to us, I suspect, because in the Bronx we were used to particular sorts of middle-class enemies—sadistic teachers, smiling bullies, cursing cab drivers, angry fathers. Even Vietnam, as distant as a half-remembered nightmare, seemed tangible, a place of jungles and sweat and blood. But this terror, and we all started to feel it in the darkness, was indefinable. It was nothing and something at the same time, real and imagined. It was a strange, unnameable sort of adult fear with a weird existential invisibility. It made me feel old—instantly, irrevocably old. It was a rush of cold air from the past or future that swept through the bowels and raced into the heart. One minute we were yawning and the next we were wide-eyed. We were caught in some strange tide—asleep, awake, our senses dulled and then alive. We felt like Rip Van Winkle in fast motion—one minute falling slowly, lethargically, into unconsciousness, and the next alert, hearts pounding, sensitive to every sound and movement around us.

By the time we calmed our friend down, most of us were holding tight to our own demons, knowing that if we let one slip out, the rest would come howling after it. We had only a little experience with drugs, but we guessed that the marijuana had been laced with PCP or opium. It was a long night, and by the next morning we all looked haggard as we leaned over the stone wall that separated the road from the precipice dropping jaggedly to the Delaware. The stone had a chalky feel, and the drop to the snaking brown river, which bent in a widening S toward lush green hills and uninhabited shores, was dizzying. No matter which way I turned my head—toward the canyon or toward the cliffs behind me—I felt off balance. As I looked into the dark circles of my friends' eyes, I thought for a moment that I saw in them an inclination to jump, a desire to meet the terror head on, a wish, perhaps, to leave the Bronx behind them suddenly and permanently. But the thought passed, a remnant of the night before, and their eyes, hawklike, turned watchful.

Once again, then, on that Friday in the middle of August, we were watchful, remembering, as we twisted along the edge of the Hawk's Nest. But once we drove beyond that road and into Barryville, we felt safe. We descended the mountain, and the road followed alongside the river. The air smelled of damp pine trees and insects. It took us about fifteen minutes to get to Dr. Duggan Road. There was already a line of cars tipsily parked on both sides of the road, leaning toward pastures and indifferent cows. We left our cars there and began to walk with thousands of others toward Route 17B and then to Max Yasgur's farm. Along the way Murphy opened a bag of marijuana, and we rolled several joints. We smoked them and rolled more. We smoked until our eyes were red and our throats burned, but nothing happened. So we smoked some more. Then somebody tasted the contents of the bag. "Hey, this tastes like oregano!" Someone else said, "Basil." And I realized that we all smelled like Italian chefs as we marched along for the remaining ten miles—hoarse, bloodshot, a dozen sober teenagers at the wildest party we had ever seen.

We never did manage to get stoned. We just missed Richie Havens, and I have a vague recollection of hearing the wild conclusion to Sly and the Family Stone's "Let me take you higher." But I do know for certain that we heard Ravi Shankar's whining sitar music fall oddly around us like sounds from another place and another time as the rain began. By the time we started to walk back to our cars to camp out near the Delaware in Yulan, the rain began to sweep in, five inches coming down in about three hours.

Soaked to the skin but still smelling of something suspiciously like spaghetti sauce, we ended up on the living room floor of Jo-Ellen's parents' house that night, and although the last words I heard were Murphy's ("We'll go back there tomorrow," and then, "Pass me another joint, eh?"), we didn't go back and spent the next two days camping alongside the Delaware River, in some no place between Woodstock and the Bronx. During the day we canoed on the river, the sounds of our voices sliding along the water from bank to bank, and at night we lay in the cool, gathering darkness, told stories, and watched fireflies flash among us. On Sunday, before we left to go back to the Bronx, to work and school, we hiked in to Shohola Brook. The brook was on the Pennsylvania side of the Delaware, on property owned by Nick Rohman. Rumor had it that a teenager had died there when he jumped from one of the cliffs on the property into the dark green waters that pooled up just beyond one of the rocky curves in the stream. So, thin and haunted, Rohman guarded his land, keeping interlopers out. We crammed ourselves into one car, which we parked about a mile away from the beginning of the faint trail that led back to the brook and the cliffs, and we snuck along the rock-strewn path, pushing limbs aside as we whispered to one another.

At a certain point the path stopped, and we had to take off our shoes and walk across the slippery boulders that rose from the water. The stream was filled with pebbles, and the water, even in August, was stinging cold. Within a few minutes we reached the cliffs and the deep pool of the brook. We found ourselves in a bower, with green limbs encircling us. The cliffs, sheer on the left bank, jutted out on the right like awkward steps into the tall trees and the mountainside. The first level, about fifteen feet above the waterline, stuck out like a presumptuous chin a few feet beyond the two upper levels. The next level was about twenty-five feet high; the highest was forty, and six to eight feet back from a clear jump down to the water.

We lay on the granite outcroppings in the sun, tossed jokes and pebbles at one another, and leaped alone and together from the first and second levels of the cliffs. The afternoon seemed to last forever. We were vaguely aware that a few miles away, half a million tired, mud-splattered young people, like us, believed that the weekend might never end. Three of us at a time held hands and jumped out from the moss-covered rocks toward the facing cliff as if we would smash ourselves in youthful exuberance against it, shattering into fragments of flesh and drops of water. But we knew that such a leap was beyond us and that we would be drawn down into the opaque depths, thrilled by both the cold and the blinding blackness.

I suppose that Shohola Brook was our Woodstock, a world separate from the Bronx and Vietnam, where time stopped, as it does occasionally, where we all—Murphy, Steve, Chris, Al, Jo-Ellen, and the rest—hung on the silky stillness of the afternoon. We knew that hundreds of thousands of young people were nearby, a community ready to believe in itself, eager to find a home. But we didn't head back to Bethel, and we didn't leap from the third tier of the cliff. It was too far back, too high, too crackling with danger. We knew that by nightfall we would be returning to the stolid Bronx and the lives we were supposed to live.

In the summer of the next year I quit my part-time job at the telephone company to travel with Jo-Ellen across the country. At the time, the journey seemed as necessary a rite of passage as baptism and holy communion, and, by the following year, holy matrimony. By the summer of 1970 we had all seen *Easy Rider* and read *On the Road*. And most of us who had come alive in the sixties felt we understood Kerouac's narrator when he said, "I'd often dreamed of going West to see the country, always vaguely planning and never taking off." Like that narrator, I had spent much of my life dreaming about "the part of my life you could call my life on the road." I felt this compulsion deep inside of me and wanted to believe that it was original in some way, but even then I had read enough to know that Ishmael and Huck had led the way and that the road had been opened for them by many others, from Odysseus to Gawain, from Marco Polo to Columbus. For me, the road may have had something to do with escape, but it had less to do with running *from* than with adventure and a crossing into meaning. The road was pure, it seemed, as Kerouac said, because in motion I could be part of the world and stand separate from it at the same time. There was a hunger in me that only the road could satisfy. My wish, I think, was to get lost enough to find myself, as Frost suggests in "Directive." Travel, I sensed, was a little bit like death—only better, of course, because it was a fictional death. It was a way of disappearing. It was something like Tom Sawyer's returning to hear his own funeral eulogy—a way of being gone without leaving forever. There is something literary about the experience as it allows you to be yourself and whatever you can make of yourself at the same time. In travel, we leave ourselves behind in the familiar world when we depart. All the known landmarks disappear, time slows, the mind is cleansed, and objects gleam anew.

So, with Jo-Ellen, I took off from the Bronx in order to leave myself behind and find some new self in the process of discovering a different landscape. It was California we sought. Everyone did then. San Francisco was the destination of the generation. It was in Berkeley that the resistance to the war was always the strongest. It was in Haight Ashbury that young people drifted away from the world of their parents. It was in City Lights Bookstore that Kerouac and Ginsberg and Ferlinghetti met. It was in the rising hills and the fog-draped bay that the Bronx seemed no longer to exist.

We headed out of New York on Route 80 and into Pennsylvania. By the time we reached Ohio, I had used up all the rolls of film I had brought with me on the wheat fields and cows along the way. Two wheat fields and two cows would have been enough, but the spaces seemed so wide and empty, the cows so incongruous, that I kept fixing my eyes on them and snapping away. I was used to the clutter and congestion of the Bronx, and the spaciousness of my own country took me by surprise. It was one thing to have Brother Placid lecture on geography or to see photographs in a textbook and another to squint into the harsh openness beyond New York State. Soon after we drove across Pennsylvania, we cut south onto Route 70 and camped in Illinois and Indiana, where the bugs were bigger and more annoying than any jokes Mark Twain had ever made about them. Around St. Louis, we crossed over the Mississippi, Twain's river, the central American artery, which emanates from the mythic heart of our culture. As Eliot said, it is a river with no beginning or ending: where it starts, it is not yet the Mississippi, and where it ends, it ceases to be the Mississippi. The river itself seems pure journey, always moving, always staying the same, always changing its shape without ever appearing to. Crossing Twain's majestic mile-wide river, then, was like crossing some imaginary line into the West, into another America, one I had read about and contemplated, but never seen.

Kansas was more than one hundred degrees in the daytime, yellow grassland undulating in a breeze that pushed air dry as dust into our mouths. We spent the night on the Osage Plains, making love under the soundless, expansive sky, fractured by starlight and our whispers. Translucent clouds floated fast over the stars, making them appear to blink. We were awakened by the wind, which rose from the prairie in a funnel of sound and gray threat. In Colorado we hiked through the Rockies and swam in an icy, quarried lake. In a small town in Utah we slept beneath a cluster of linden trees in a park on the edge of the town square. Good winds seemed to follow us, even into Las Vegas, where we won $105 at the roulette table, giving us enough to eat out in San Francisco when we arrived the next day.

We fell in love with San Francisco and knew right away that we would start our lives together there, at the farthest distance from the Bronx we could manage while still remaining in our own country. San Francisco became a separate world for us, where the hills abandoned themselves to the windswept bay and fog shrouded the Golden Gate Bridge every morning, where the colors of the Victorian houses glinted in the afternoon sunlight, and in the evening the chill wind had the taste of salt spray to it. It was a city of dreams for us, partly because it was so beautiful but mainly because we found ourselves there together. The Bronx seemed old and sadly worn, but San Francisco was young and filled with life.

We spent a few days in Berkeley, where in 1970 the decade of the sixties still felt young, as if the throbbing anger and wild passion were just beginning. Walking along Telegraph Avenue, which stretched from the campus to the mean streets of Oakland, we felt ourselves in a landscape as strangely alive and exotic as Bethel the summer before. We spent time sitting on the marble steps that led down to Sproul Plaza, listening to X Swami X recite his revolutionary lyrics, and I would watch the sunlight play on the cords of Jo-Ellen's long blonde hair.

We drifted back and forth between San Francisco and Berkeley, strolling through Golden Gate Park and Chinatown, walking along Muir Beach, winding our way through the hills of Oakland. The need to run was strong in me, and the Bay Area seemed like a destination different from the Bronx—open and free. I didn't think of New York's Chinatown or Rockaway Beach or Central Park. Instead, I felt, perhaps as all young people feel in such situations, that I had found another land, that I had discovered a new territory.

And in a sense I had, for such territory is always new for the one doing the discovering. I thought I had left the Bronx far behind me. I was too young, though, to understand then what I had actually stumbled upon. Hardly anyone is ever old enough at the right time. I sensed that I had not come in a direct line to some uncharted point, but rather had circled back to something that I had always had in my possession. I had an intuition that a sense of place was more deeply rooted in the heart and the imagination than it was in the physical facts of the landscape. Place was a collection of people and experiences and memories. When Jo-Ellen turned her face toward mine and smiled quizzically at me, I felt an odd sense of longing—for what I had, for what could not last forever. But I felt that I had arrived where I had started and knew the place, knew my place, for the first time.

Still, it wasn't easy to leave San Francisco and turn east, back toward New York and my last year of college, toward what seemed like a past life just when a new one was beginning, but we drove back through Salt Lake City. We floated like dead men on the fly-specked expanse of water, salt stinging our eyes and pores, and spent the night in a motel operated by a man who looked too keenly like Norman Bates. It seemed as if we were going in the wrong direction. Through Yellowstone and the Grand Tetons I dreamt of mountains and bears. Through Nebraska and Iowa I dreamt of corn fields, and in Pennsylvania I began to dream again of the Bronx, the exhausted faces, the colorless apartment buildings, the life that I had already left behind.

The Bronx we returned to seemed dingier than it had in the early summer. Graffiti covered buildings and hallways, buses and subways. Darby O'Gill's was damp and filled with shadows. My parents' apartment at 2902 Grand Concourse was smaller than I had remembered. Fewer people were on the streets after dark, and the faces were no longer familiar ones. In my absence the Bronx had become some other place, an exaggeration of my memory of it. Or perhaps it had not changed at all, but rather I had already departed. I was back in San Francisco with Jo-Ellen, beginning a new life, and the next year seemed surreal because I felt as if I were living in my own past.

At the same time, there seemed to be a new lambency to the Bronx. As I walked from one street to another, I knew that it was no longer my home, as it had once been—dwelling place, world, village, everything I knew. But the Bronx River still flowed though my imagination, as did Harris Field and Kevin Flynn and Dennis Murphy. Rip had disappeared from my view. So had Jimmy Bufano and Tommy Murray and Gary Delano. Sarah's Candy Store was gone. The playground at St. Philip Neri was no longer mine. But they were all there, more vividly, perhaps, because they weren't. The Bronx had a new, ghostly life because I realized that I had left for good, and by the time I returned, time would have changed us both.

•••••

The Bronx is real.

—Don DeLillo, *Underworld*

It's hot enough for scores of people to be on the streets, but not in the numbers that will be there, of course, by the end of June. Then, in the hot months of 1995, when the kids finish with school for the year and the junkies scratch their way out of dank, unlit hallways, the streets and parks will support a varied picture of life—sweat-glistening bodies slapping against one another on the basketball courts; long, liquid looks from drooping heads on the stoops; young mothers pushing strollers; the unemployed hanging on street corners. It will be a picture of desire and boredom, not one fighting for dominance over the other, but coexisting, lazily, like two old lovers.

The Hunts Point section of the South Bronx is not that far from where Jonas Bronck built his stone house and barns three and a half centuries ago. The bucolic setting that he described with such hopefulness is not visible anywhere in this bleak landscape. Three hundred fifty years is a long time, but the kind of change this part of the Bronx has undergone seems like the sort of metamorphosis only geologic time could create. It reminds me of Michael Stephens's description of the Bronx in *Green Dreams:* "funky, corroded, broken down, downtrodden, almost like a war zone, brick-piled, lot-strewn, garbage-infested, crime-filled, even evil."

Evil and danger seem to lurk everywhere, so much so that I feel a hollowness in my stomach as soon as I exit the number 6 train at Hunts Point Avenue and breathe in the acrid smell of heat and despair that collects under the Bruckner Expressway. The air is swollen and still, stale with industrial sweat, anger, and fear. One study showed that residents of some parts of Hunts Point have less than one chance in twenty of dying of natural causes. The *New York Times* reported, "In basic ways, portions of the Hunts Point section of the southeast Bronx have ceased to be part of New York City." The reporter was referring to the disappearance of police protection, garbage collection, and certain typical citizen obligations: "Nearly everything [there] seems touched by lawlessness." In Hunts Point, drugs are rampant, prostitution is commonplace, and violence is expected. This part of the Bronx is the heart of darkness in America, the symbol of urban decay and all that is rotting in Harlem and East St. Louis, in the slums of New Orleans or Los Angeles.

Every road here seems to lead to the Hunts Point Terminal Market. The market brings the trucks, the many glass repair companies that serve the trucks, and the prostitutes who line the streets night and day serve both the glass workers and the truckers, as well as the businessmen who occasionally dare to drive down one of the side streets. Hunts Point Market, which sits on a peninsula of marsh land between the Bronx River and the East River, was developed in the late 1960s. Now, it looks like a military installation, trucks wheezing through the big gates day and night. In the early morning hours they roll in from all over the country with fresh produce. In the late afternoon grocers from all over the city come to buy fruits and vegetables for their stores.

At first glance, Hunts Point appears to be exactly what its reputation suggests: a nightmare world of crack addicts, prostitutes, welfare mothers, Neanderthal glass workers, scurrilous truckers— a Tower of Babel imagined by Federico Fellini. The area seems to be an emblem of all that is bad in the Bronx multiplied, exaggerated, until those who live here have only three choices: to fall like Joseph Conrad's Kurtz into the open arms of the horror, to lose all hope and live in blank-eyed despair, or to long for some distant escape. This is a place to induce dreams of running, a breathless, never-ending running, as long as those streets stay behind you. It makes me wonder what has drawn me back to the Bronx, what would draw anyone who didn't have to be here back to such a place.

So it seems strange to me that Steven Sapp would return, like Huck heading back instead of out. But the twenty-eight-year-old Sapp, who grew up in the Forest Projects about ten minutes from here, came back to the Bronx in 1991, a few years after he graduated from Bard College. At Bard, an unusual place for a Black kid from the Bronx to end up going to school, Sapp studied playwriting, but those five years at the posh private school in the Hudson Valley taught him more about himself than they did about dramaturgy. He spent those years caught between two worlds. At Bard he was smart, but Black. At home he sounded White to his friends. The first play he wrote at Bard, *Purgatory*, captures his feeling of dislocation.

He doesn't say exactly why he returned. Family. Friends. His past. Perhaps he came back because for him this part of the Bronx *is* the territories; it is more truly the wilderness than any portion of the Hudson Valley ever will be. Now, along with three other paint-splattered, smiling young people—Paul Lipson, Mildred Ruiz, and Maria Torres—he is cofounder of the Point Community Development Corporation. They have a ten-year lease on a building at 940 Garrison Avenue, in the heart of Hunts Point. Formerly a currency warehouse, the Point is a brick-walled compound that will have an open-air market, a theater in the round, stalls for local businesses, and an eatery. The four founders have a simple dream—to have a community center where the arts, culture, business, and social services converge. The Point will have a barber shop, a Spanish restaurant, a sculptor, a fashion designer, counseling services, dance classes, art instruction, dramatic presentations. Twelve thousand square feet of murals and gardens, it will be a Globe Theater in a section of the city that many residents would prefer to forget.

While Steven tells me about his dreams for the Point as we sit on top of recently cut stumps in one of the walled courtyard areas of the property, his eyes grow wide and his ebony skin looks polished in the sunlight. A silver earring, with the masks of comedy and tragedy cut into it, flutters on his left ear under a black baseball cap. Behind him, a white butterfly rises and falls on a tremulous breeze. "A decade ago," he says, "Hunts Point was burnt out. When we moved in here last September, there was a whole line of people in broad daylight—all sorts of people, in suits, in rags, White guys, Blacks, Puerto Ricans, men and women—in line to buy drugs as if this was a department store." He pauses and rubs his fingers along the outlines of the peace sign on his bracelet. "When I was a kid growing up here, I wasn't the smartest one. There were kids who were much smarter. Some of them were so smart they thought they were smart enough to beat this place at its own game. But nobody can beat this place in that way. If I've learned anything, I've learned that it has to be beaten from the inside, individually, by opposition. If you take that knowledge and you run—well, I couldn't do that."

Steven wants me to see what the Point might mean in that area, so he guides me around the streets, down to the market and back. Besides the myriad glass repair garages and the dominant market, there are three other landmarks within a few square blocks. The American Bank Note Company Building stands monumental, vacant, a faded beauty. The Spofford Juvenile Detention Facility stands pale and ugly, throbbing with life behind its barbed wire and barred windows. Corpus Christi Monastery, which takes up acres along Lafayette Avenue, is silent, separated from the dirty streets by walls thirty feet high. Cloistered Dominican nuns sitting quietly behind those walls in the shade of a big white birch tree must occasionally hear youngsters scrawling graffiti on the red iron entrance doors and note the sound of heels clicking on the pavement a few feet beyond their touch.

But as I put on my "train face" for the ride on the subway through Harlem and back into Manhattan, I am not thinking about the residents of Spofford or the ghosts in the American Bank Note Building or Dominican nuns. Nor am I wondering about the lives behind the exhausted, spiritless faces across the subway aisle from me. Instead, I'm seeing the hands of Steven Sapp, covered in the dust of sheet rock. I hear the sounds of saws and hammers, of stories being told and laughter. I see dancers and actors. And it doesn't seem impossible to conceive that Jonas Bronck's vision of "unlimited opportunities" could find life, once again, even in such a place, that even the oldest stories can be rewritten.

Shohola Creek, *the* Bronx, *and* Home

> *"I just realized something," he said, "I don't have an*
> *address. I don't live anywhere."*
> —Walker Percy, *The Second Coming*

> *Stop searching. Face the earth where you can.*
> *Literally speaking, it's all you have to go on.*
> —Richard Ford, *The Sportswriter*

Rumor had it that the Rolling Stones would be there Saturday night. I guess the theory was that they would be flown in by helicopter. Mick Jagger—looking just like Rip now, I imagined—would slither down like a snake onto the stage as the crowd screamed out the lyrics to "Get Off of My Cloud." But the only one from the past who flew in to perform that night was Arlo Guthrie, singing about "Los Angeleez."

Cars were parked next to the open fields on Dr. Duggan Road, and on Route 17B small groups of people straggled along in the twilight. A narrow blacktop road led to the site of the festival, and by the time we reached that road, the darkness was black and complete. Each sound—a voice, a cough, a twig cracking under a boot heel—became a point of light. Every few minutes a shadow would emerge from the night, degrees of blackness disappearing into one another. Occasionally, a four-wheeler driven by a local police officer or an emergency vehicle would come up the road, shining its headlights onto the oncoming people, turning them into shades. Then the dark would fall again, stronger than any light, and only the voices were left, rustling like dry leaves in the wind.

About two miles up there was a city of lights on Max Yasgur's old place, tents and campers and open fires softly illuminating the muddy paths that encircled the area and led down to the bandstand. It looked like a ramshackle suburb of about twenty thousand souls. Again, twenty-five years later twelve of us had come in two cars, but this time a few were young children, exhausted from hiking in and being up too late past their bedtime. With the stage right below us, music drifting faintly in our direction, eight of us had to leave, envious for a moment of the four men who stayed behind.

It seemed fitting, though, that Woodstock in 1994 was much the same for me as it had been in 1969, a brief encounter, a distant music, a memory before it had enough time to be an experience. It was a reunion in Bethel, but for me it was a chance to see my oldest son, Shane, whom I hadn't seen in eight months since he had moved to New York City. He came up from the city with his girlfriend, and it was in those dark miles we walked that I saw our lives, now separate, once again joined. Twenty-five years ago I had been his age, in this place, and the present and the past appeared to be seamless for a moment.

The place where Shohola Creek empties into the Delaware River was once a spot where geese gathered, and thus the Indian tribes in the area named the region *Shohola*, "where the geese rest." Certainly it is restful, with its rolling hills and rippling streams, but it is not a place for sleep, but for wakefulness. "To be awake," as Thoreau said, "is to be alive." And this place is filled with "infinite expectation."

It is also a place that echoes with memories as Jo-Ellen, two of our sons, and I stumble along the narrow path that descends toward the cliffs at the silent center of the creek. We've come here with friends and their children, about the same number of people who trudged along the same tapering, rocky path to the water's edge twenty-five years ago.

For a moment I see myself as Rip Van Winkle after a long sleep, opening my dream-dazed eyes to find that nothing has changed and everything has. Standing there, looking at the jagged cliffs and the dark green pool of water beneath them, I feel as if I have returned to a dreamily familiar place. It is silent and still enough to make me wonder if I can start all over again—no memories, just dreams. But as I look around me and see most of what I love in the world, how could I wish to stop time or begin it all over? Time, it seems, is a circle that we travel around and around, wayfarers not by choice but by fate, inching along, pushed by experience and memory out into the world and back into ourselves. Perhaps the past should not be escaped too readily. In this place, like the Bronx, a certain kind of knowledge seems inescapable. It is here and now, at Shohola Creek, that the world is alert to both the past and the future, the present holding on tenuously, as it always does, in the sound of children's laughter or the murmuring song of a stream.

There was a grove of trees near the reservoir adjacent to Harris Field in the Bronx. My father took me there when I was very small. He called it the "cool spot," and I remembered it by that name when I got older and went there to feel a breeze off the water on those stifling summer days when the air was too thick to breathe. I always associated the place with my father, his eyes as sad and seeking as Columbus's. I would sit in the shade and try to imagine the reservoir stretching out to the Hudson River a few miles to the west. At times, I would sit there, leaning back against the ridged trunk of a slippery elm, and daydream about launching myself on a raft on the Bronx River, passing Fordham Road and West Farms Square, floating under the Bruckner Expressway, drifting past Hunts Point and out into the East River, the Long Island Sound, and the mysterious world beyond.

The Bronx River flows directly through the center of the Bronx; and where Owen, my youngest son, and I stand in the Botanical Gardens, we are in the geographic middle of the borough. Here, it is peaceful and serene. The distant thrum of traffic is no louder than the sound of our own blood beating in our ears. There is the damp smell of thick foliage and the murmur of a waterfall not far away. Bluebirds alight on branches, and chipmunks dart into the underbrush. When I was his age, I tell Owen, this was the closest thing I had to a garden and river, really a dark stream that we sat by and only dared to swim in when the thought of scum and snapping turtles was not enough to dissuade us from a belief in our own courage or the invincibility of our immune systems. I tell him that my most vivid memory of the spot where we now stand is of Herman Bosenbrook, a superintendent's son, who was older than I was and had a pockmarked face and thick, purple lips, and who dove into those tarry depths. He shamed the rest of us into jumping, but he dove, and then he sat on one of the big rocks that lined the banks and opened bottles of soda for us with his teeth. He placed the bottle cap against his back teeth and jerked the glass forward. Then he reclined on the boulder like a Viking warrior, ugly but without fear, and tossed the empties into the stream.

Owen stares into the water as if he expects to see a bottle spring cheerfully to the surface to confirm my tale, and I see him as he sees himself in the river looking up at Herman Bosenbrook, a bottle cap stuck between his meaty lips.

.....

The last time I saw the Bronx it seemed crammed with buildings and cars, people and memories. I couldn't understand how it made it from one day to the next. The Bronx reminded me of E. B. White's remark about the city in general—"It is a miracle that New York works at all. The whole thing is implausible." The smells of garbage and exhaust were everywhere, but people breathed them in as if they were all part of the clean air of New Hampshire. Barbed wire glistened in the moonlight, but young boys and girls still sauntered down the streets as if their virtue assured their safety. Cars double-parked along the side streets, and horns honked every few seconds. But teenage girls jumped rope on the Concourse, clapping hands and singing some street verse as if the entire city were a play-ground put in place for their enjoyment.

The whole thing, everything about the Bronx, seemed implausi-ble. Too many people, too much graffiti, drugs, violence, insolence, noise. But the mail got delivered, and people fell in love. Shoppers picked through the fruit at the vegetable stands, and young boys chased each other with fury and laughter around fire hydrants. At night, the heavens turned charcoal, and people gazed out of their windows at the stars flickering in their small patch of sky and at the few pedestrians straggling along toward bars or apartments. Then, as the city turned toward darkness and sleep, the Bronx seemed al-most magnificent in its preposterousness, for each resident knew that the place would awaken the next morning the same—as unrea-sonable and excessive as Manhattan, but without the museums or theaters or bookstores. It would be there once again, bland and sin-ister at the same time; some would dream that they were not there, and others that they had returned from a long and difficult journey.

My dreams of the Bronx are often filled with running. One dream repeated itself for years. I am running down Bainbridge Avenue to Briggs Avenue toward P.S. 8 and Mosholu Parkway. Along the way

I see Loretta and Brother Bruce, my mother and father, Mother Concepta, Tommy Murray and Little Man, Jimmy Bufano, Gary Delano,
Al, Fitz, Murphy, Elka, Molly, Marguerite Young. Face after face
floats from hallways and basements. They are all clear-eyed, ebul-
lient—except for Rip, who is slouching along the railing, which has
been furrowed with paint and rust. He looks middle aged and
heavy lidded, as if his dreams, which he once thought would sup-
plant the world, had betrayed him. But as I stand in front of him, he
looks up and through some deep concentration sheds a quarter of a
century. The wrinkles disappear, his hair flashes out into a tangle of
curls, his shoulders straighten, and a bemused look teases the corners of his mouth.

Then I awaken, unsure for a moment which memory of Rip is
the true one, which picture of the Bronx is real. Which form of *running*, I wonder, do I most truly remember? Is it the running to
candy store and playground, toward the goal line on Harris Field,
toward my mother's arms, toward love? Or is it the running from
the grey and brown brick, the world that seemed too solid and un-
moving and at the same time too surely crumbling? Then, fully
awake, I sometimes imagine I am running, still. And my youthful
dream of Columbus seems, at that moment, both necessary and
foolish, both true and naïve. It is my father's past and my sons' future. It is Steven Sapp and Mrs. Murther and Mother David. It is a
dream in which stillness and movement are one and the same,
where loss and discovery intersect like lines drawn on a map. For
me, the Bronx was filled with books and archangels, Spaldeens and
rosary beads, tall buildings and an implicit horizon beyond. The
Bronx is a story that shapes me as I have shaped it.

It is Fourth of July weekend in 1995. We are visiting my son Shane,
who is now twenty-one years old and has a brand new baby girl of
his own, Shana Michele. He lives in Brooklyn, not that far from

Grove Street, where his grandfather grew up three-quarters of a century ago.

Today, Shane gently rocks the carriage in which Shana sleeps. Ian, Owen, and I stand beside them as we watch a basketball game on West Fourth Street in Greenwich Village. I'm not sure what my sons are thinking at this moment. They might be imagining themselves in that full-court game. Their faces are inscrutable, but perhaps, like me, they are imagining the four of us playing here together, knowing each other's moves so well that we can pass the ball without even looking because the other will be there, knowing when to pick and roll, when to switch on defense, when to get out of the way so that the other can shoot.

I look back and see Jo-Ellen is walking up the street with a shopping bag in her hand, walking toward us, looking for us in the crowd. And in my daydreams I feel fully awake, far from home, but at home. Like this game we watch, home is a thing that moves and shifts. It is memory and experience and desire. It is place and no place. It is crowded with faces and filled with voices, and it is as mute as a dream.

Across the river is Brooklyn. A few miles to the north is the Bronx. Across the Verrazzano Bridge to the south is Virginia Beach, where I live, a day's drive away. These places are where we face the world, but our homes are connected to our journeys, our memories, our dreams, and we run from their predatory grasp and toward their welcoming arms.